The Jesus Factor in Justice *and* Peacemaking

THEOLOGICAL POSTINGS SERIES

Many faithful Christians seek to be informed about current events and apply their faith convictions to our complex and conflicted world. However, most have a hard time finding space in their busy schedules for scholarly inquiry and also experience a great deal of theological writing to be difficult to understand and apply. Many do not need to be convinced to take theology seriously so much as to be provided theological writing that meets them halfway—and provides them with access to the relevance of Christianity's biblical-theological resources.

The concise volumes in the Theological Postings Series seek to meet this need. These books are grounded in solid scholarship but wear it lightly. They connect the biblical narrative and theological tradition with contemporary issues. Thus they provide an "exegesis" of the contemporary situation as well as of the biblical world and of the churches in history.

The Theological Postings Series is currently edited by Ted Grimsrud and C. Norman Kraus and released by Cascadia Publishing House LLC.

1. The Jesus Factor in Justice and Peacemaking
   C. Norman Kraus, 2011

The Jesus Factor in Justice *and* Peacemaking

C. Norman Kraus

Foreword by Howard Zehr

Theological Postings Series, Volume 1

Cascadia
Publishing House
Telford, Pennsylvania

Cascadia Publishing House LLC orders, information, reprint permissions:
contact@cascadiapublishinghouse.com
1-215-723-9125
126 Klingerman Road, Telford PA 18969
www.CascadiaPublishingHouse.com

The Jesus Factor
Copyright © 2011 by Cascadia Publishing House
a division of Cascadia Publishing House LLC, Telford, PA 18969
All rights reserved.
Library of Congress Catalog Number: 2011018975
ISBN 13: 978-1-931038-82-9; **ISBN 10:** 1-931038-82-1
Book design by Cascadia Publishing House
Cover art, "Molitva" (Prayer), by Marko Zivkovic, Osijek, Croatia, internationally known art teacher at the University of Osijek.
Used by permission.

The paper used in this publication is recycled and meets the minimum requirements of American National Standard for Information Sciences—Permanence of Paper for Printed Library Materials, ANSI Z39.48-1984.

All Bible quotations are used by permission, all rights reserved and unless otherwise noted or occasionally slightly paraphrased by the author, who is a Greek scholar, are from *The New Revised Standard Version of the Bible*, copyright 1989, by the Division of Christian Education of the National Council of the Churches of Christ in the USA.

Library of Congress Cataloguing-in-Publication Data
Kraus, C. Norman (Clyde Norman), 1924-
  The Jesus factor in justice and peacemaking / by C. Norman Kraus ; foreword by Howard Zehr.
   p. cm. -- (Theological postings series ; 1)
  Summary: "This book addresses the impact of Jesus on the practice of conflict resolution interventions, such as restorative justice, mediation, peacebuilding, and trauma healing." "[summary]"--Provided by publisher.
  Includes bibliographical references (p.   ).
  ISBN-13: 978-1-931038-83-6 (5.5 x 8.5 trade pbk. : alk. paper)
  ISBN-10: 1-931038-83-X (5.5 x 8.5 trade pbk. : alk. paper)
  1. Jesus Christ--Teachings. 2. Jesus Christ--Influence. 3. Conflict management--Biblical teaching. 4. Justice--Religious aspects--Christianity. 5. Peace--Religious aspects--Christianity. I. Title.
  BS2415.K65 2011
  261.8'73--dc23
                    2011018975

16 15 14 13 12 11   10 9 8 7 6 5 4 3 2

To my children, some of whom have turned to other religious paths for inspiration.

CONTENTS

Foreword by Howard Zehr 11
Author's Preface 13
Introduction 15

1 WHY NOT THE BIBLE • 23
Authority vs. Experience
From Aphorism to Practice
Jesus' New Paradigm: Which Jesus?
Postscript for Evangelicals

2 JESUS AND RELIGIOUS PLURALISM • 35
Christianity Among World Religions
Jesus and Religion
Jesus and Temple Judaism
The Jesus Paradigm and Global Cultures
Re-scribing the Exclusive Paradigm

3 THE JESUS STYLE OF PEACEMAKING • 50
Lord Jesus, Lord Buddha
Jesus and Pacifism
A Jesus Style
Reconciliation and Shalom

4 FRAMING JESUS' MESSAGE • 63
Kingship—the Frame for Jesus' Message
What Kind of a Kingdom

God's "Wrath"
Recognizing the Culture Gap

5 JESUS AND ISRAEL'S VIEW OF GOD • 74
God as "Almighty"
Jesus' View of God as "Abba"
Jesus' View of God's Power and Justice
God's Forgiveness

6 JESUS, LAW, AND JUSTICE • 86
Jesus and Mosaic Tradition
Law and Love
"But I Say to You"

7 "VINDICATION": RETALIATION OR RESTORATION? • 95
Overview of Terms
Jesus' View of Retaliation
But Coerced Retribution?

8 JESUS AND MODERN PEACEMAKING • 106
Bridging the Culture Gap
Jesus and Modern Peacemaking

Notes 120
The Author 125

Foreword

The relationship between Jesus and peace has been a confused and controversial subject. Was Jesus essentially a peacemaker? Does the Jesus approach to peacemaking apply to social-political peacemaking or primarily to personal peace? Did he advocate nonviolence as well as non-coercion? Is his way the only way to peace? How do we reconcile Jesus' teachings on peace with God's judgment? What kind of power does Jesus claim?

Can we learn anything from a figure who lived in a context so different from our own?

How do Jesus' teachings relate to teachings from other faith traditions?

Is there a tension between modern, evidence-based practice and Jesus' teachings? Does Jesus have any relevance for practical efforts toward peace and justice?

In this surprisingly short but sophisticated book, Kraus tackles some of the most complicated and controversial issues in biblical interpretation with clarity, simplicity, and practical relevance. He does argue that Jesus' way is a way of peace, though it is not the only approach and does not rule out all coercion.

Moreover, the way to peace cannot be understood as a series of rules, or interpretations of a few passages, or as dogma to be imposed. Rather, Jesus offers an overall "gestalt"—a pattern of thinking grounded in a vision of right relationships and the importance of respectful dialogue, a peace to be realized not *"through hegemonic religious domination but through God's offer of conflict transformation across religious boundaries!"*

For the past fifteen years I have been part of the Center for Justice & Peacebuilding (CJP) at Eastern Mennonite University, a practice-oriented graduate program that brings practitioners from dozens of countries and many faiths together to learn from each other. My own area of work is in restorative justice, but our team includes colleagues with backgrounds in conflict transformation, trauma healing, organizational health, and community development. We see these fields, and others, as essential parts of peacebuilding.

Although we are explicitly Christian, we acknowledge the contributions of various religious faiths and seek to create a hospitable climate of respectful, open dialogue in which all of us who participate learn from one another. In his Preface, Kraus notes that this book was originally envisioned for us at CJP and our diverse community. Although the manuscript has gone through many transformations since that original vision and is now relevant to a much wider audience, I believe he has accomplished his original goal. This book will be a real asset to our CJP community of learning and practice.

If you are a Christian interested in peace, if you are a Christian justice or peace practitioner, if you are Buddhist or Hindu or Jewish and interested in understanding connections between your own faith and Christian approaches to peace—then this book is for you.

—*Howard Zehr, Harrisonburg, Virginia*
  Professor of Restorative Justice, Center for Justice and Peacebuilding, Eastern Mennonite University

AUTHOR'S PREFACE

This book was envisioned originally with a specific audience in mind, namely, the cross-cultural international inter-religious group studying at the Center for Justice and Peacebuilding at Eastern Mennonite University. That group is highly diversified, representing many nationalities, cultures, and religions, and it cannot be expected that they will be intimately acquainted with all complexities of American religious culture. Most of them, including Americans from various Christian backgrounds, have little knowledge of the biblical or theological grounding of Christian concepts of peace and peacemaking.

Religious figures from the Hindu Gandhi to the most rightwing evangelical Christians may lay claim to the words of Paul in Ephesians 2:14, "He [Jesus] is our peace [who] has . . . broken down the dividing wall, that is, the hostility between us," but their interpretations of the meaning and implications differ widely. With this in mind I have tried to locate my approach within the wide variety and nuances in the North American Christian understanding of peace, at the same time recognizing the significant contributions that other religious traditions have made.

As the months of writing and rewriting, which eventually turned into several years, passed I began to focus the approach more directly on the American situation, realizing that the United States religious scene is a virtual potpourri of religious concepts. So what role does the first-century Jesus play in contemporary Christian understandings of peacemaking? How do his concepts of peace relate to those of the Vietnamese Buddhist Thich Nat Hahn, for example, who shows great reverence for Jesus in his quest for peace? More specifically, how does Jesus factor into the politicized process of professional conflict transformation and peacebuilding? That is the subject of this book.

—C. Norman Kraus
 Harrisonburg, Virginia

Introduction

Jesus is called the "Prince of peace," and perhaps his most oft-quoted saying is "Blessed are the peacemakers." But just what his relationship and relevance is to the modern peacemaking process is confused. Even in the West where Christianity has had a long tradition the impression many people have of Jesus is a bit wimpish and pious, if they have any image at all.

Brad Stine, an American "evangelical comedian," has organized GodMen, an evangelical movement which, he says, is to help men reclaim their masculinity in the church. In an interview on ABC News he observed, "Churchgoers are taught to reflect the meek and mild image of Jesus Christ. If someone strikes you on the right check, turn to him the other also, churches often preach." Then he continues, "One God-Men attendant says he's running out of cheeks." And Stine adds, "A meek and mild Jesus . . . eventually is a bore!"[1]

More often one gets the impression that Jesus is merely a source of spiritual inspiration and encouragement and has little or nothing to do with the peacemaking process. Indeed, one might get the impression from songs like the "Battle Hymn of the Republic" that Jesus, like Lady Liberty, is at the forefront of battle in the fight for freedom and democratic order. He becomes the symbol of peace and security through violent resistance to the enemies of freedom!

Perhaps we should not be surprised at this kind of confused reading. Already in Jesus' own day his presence and ministry often raised conflict and was often threatening. There is a story of this kind recorded in Matthew 8 that epitomizes the ambiguity of Jesus' peacemaking. When Jesus visited the town of Gadara on the eastern side of the Sea of Galilee, he was approached by two fearful, hostile men who, according to the diagnosis of the day, were possessed by evil spirits. They were kept from disturbing the peace of the town by ostracism and when necessary put in chains. These men challenged his jurisdiction shouting, "[Jesus] Son of God, what do we have in common? Leave us alone!" And when Jesus transformed the anger and conflict in their lives, it caused consternation and fear in the town. Peace for two anguished men upset the political and economic status quo.

Yet the impression persists that Jesus represents a saintly, nonviolent, pacifistic ideal that does not and probably cannot, deal with the realism of our violent modern world. He was an idealist whose teachings and example, as praiseworthy as they are, really belong to another world. A few days after the 9-11 terrorist bombing of the International Trade Center in New York City, I remember reading in a prominent newspaper that "This is no time for the president to ask the question, what would Jesus do!" Perhaps this was because in the 1999 presidential campaign he had avowed that Christ was his "favorite philosopher."

At the time this seemed like a clear reflection of the national mood, but now years later after all the carnage, death, increased insecurity, and continuing political turmoil one might be pardoned for asking whether it might not have been a good idea after all! Jesus' advice on peacemaking would not have been an immediate pragmatic political solution to the developing crisis, but clearly he would have pointed the national reaction in a different direction than vengeful war.

I remember thinking at the time how much the Middle Eastern faces of Osama bin Laden and his followers might resemble the faces of both the first-century Jesus and the insurgents from Galilee and Judea who violently disagreed with him. They were called zealots and were viewed by the Romans as terrorists and bandits. Two of them were crucified at the same time with Jesus, one on either side. And now, two thousand years later the United States was preparing to respond to a terrorist attack much as the Romans would have reacted to first-century Jewish insurgents whom scholars call Zealots. What would Jesus advise? What kind of a person was he? Some have claimed that he was a covert Zealot, others that he was an absolute pacifist. If the president had counseled with him, what might he have recommended?

Peacebuilding in our modern context is a social-political process with clear political dimensions that ironically lead to "culture wars" among Christians. Claiming to be citizens of Christ's spiritual "kingdom," they fight over political ideology and practice, and the question becomes how God's kingdom rule is related to the social-political process. The sanctions and motivation for kingdom and power-politics responses diverge widely! The peace of God's kingdom is not brought about by power politics, whether religious or secular, and the question becomes how citizens of the kingdom are to be political peacemakers, if, indeed, they should attempt it at all. Is the peacemaking paradigm to be one of political tolerance? Compromise? Cautious cooperation? Resistance? Passive submission?

Further, Jesus was operating with quite different cultural and political assumptions than we in the modern democratic world. For him citizenship was first and primarily a covenantal relationship with God. True human identity was found as God's children, not as Roman citizens. *Citizens* of the nonviolent kingdom of God were *subjects* under the violent, self-serving power of Rome. Their peacemaking responsibilities as Roman subjects stemmed from their transcendent citizenship, not their political classification. Thus his words to them concerning peacemaking speak in terms of responsible, compassionate relationships under God's covenant.

But before we pursue this question further, the question of "why *Jesus*?" looms in front of us. It also points to a prior question: Why refer to a religious norm at all? Peacemaking as practiced in the civil and political spheres is fundamentally a secular discipline, and the qualifying degrees for its practice are gained in the study of sociological and psychological disciplines. What do religious leaders bring to the process? What is the source and authentication of their contributions to the peacemaking process? And how does their religious contribution impact the concept and processes of peacemaking?

Also, if we raise the religious question, which religion should we appeal to for definition? Conflict transformation and peacebuilding have clearly crossed cultural and religious borders, as indeed they should. As a matter of fact most present peacebuilding programs are a blend of Hebrew-Christian, Hindu, Buddhist, Muslim, and secular social values. That is the whole point of dealing with diversity that causes violent conflict between cultures.

I would argue that the very nature of the peace quest requires it to be dialogical. There is a common *human* element, which the Hebrew-Christian tradition describes as "the image of God," to which all religious faiths appeal. The possibility and desirability of dialogue is based on this common element, which Christianity understands as the creative gift of God. And for genuine dialogue to happen the unique contribution of each cultural religious experience must be recognized, which in turn implies that the claims of each party need to be clearly understood, evaluated, and shared.

For example, as Thich Nhat Hahn's sympathetic attempt to understand and compare Jesus to Buddha implies, Buddhists dare not simply assume the superiority of the Buddha's teaching and example without further question. And Christians dare not dogmatically insist on the uncompromising preeminence of Jesus' teaching—especially not when their interpretations of his life and significance are in such intramural conflict. Christian peacemakers must be willing to non-defensively face the historical reality of Jesus as peacemaker and the difficulty of applying his example and teaching that causes such diversity among themselves.

Some would argue that to try to sort out and define specific religious sources simply raises red flags. That to meld a compromised "spiritual" approach under a secular banner is the most politic way to achieve peace. But given the resurgence of religious ideology as a power broker on the world scene, it seems doubtful that this approach can succeed. Especially so since both the dominant secular philosophy of the West and the competing religious tradition of Islamic cultures are enforced by military violence. I would argue that sincere dialogue which seeks to both recognize and respect the complementary strengths and weaknesses of the religious paradigms can move us beyond the violence of the present world situation.

So what is distinctive about the life and message of Jesus that prompts the title of this book? Why Jesus and not Lord Krishna from the Bhagavad Gita, or the sutras of the Buddha? With the globalization of communication and travel, the peace conversation has become increasingly multi-religious in character. Gandhi, Bonhoeffer, the Dali Lama, Martin Luther King Jr., Thich Nhat Hahn, Desmond Tutu, all belong at the peace table. Each represents a distinct religious cultural tradition and viewpoint that can bring depth to the discussion. My aim is to join the dialogue as a committed follower of Jesus, the "Prince of peace," but with deep appreciation for the truth held in common by the diverse religious cultures. With the resurgent interest in the possibilities of forgiveness and reconciliation as a political means to establish social justice, Jesus' teaching and example gain new relevance.

I will point out that the very concepts of reconciliation and restorative justice emerge from the Hebrew religious ideology and Jesus' view of peace as *shalom*—a just and harmonious social relation based on *agape* (compassionate empathy). This differs from those religious cultures stemming from ancient Hindu and Chinese concepts of *shanti* and *wa*, or the self-cultivation of inner harmony and contentment that undergird social equilibrium. Each has its own definition and logic for attaining peaceful community; I hasten to add that these different concepts of peace, though not contradictory, do influence our understanding of peace and the procedures of peacemaking.

Jesus does not spell out a political casuistry for arriving at an ideally just order, nor does he guarantee political success for peacemakers who follow his way. The peacemaker's job is not to create a utopia. Rather, Jesus represents a consistently nonviolent, but not non-coercive, way to transform the conflict endemic to human society. Peace for him is a dynamic relationship in which differences, disagreements, and offenses are not settled by appeal to violent power but by appeal to the original justice implied in creation—what the writers of *Ecclesiasticus* and *Proverbs* call "wisdom" that guides creation and human affairs. He does not represent a political way to create an immediate righteous social order of static perfection but a way to move human history toward its transformation, which he assures us will come in God's time. His is a politics of hope not of immediate success.

Finally, an appeal to the Jesus factor does not introduce a rational silver bullet that will dissolve all moral dissonance and resolve all our moral dilemmas. As Mark Lilla points out in his *The Stillborn God*, the major weakness of nineteenth-century religious liberalism was its over-simplification of the human problem and its optimism based on human reason and technology. In this it failed to represent the sober realism of the warnings of Jesus. But we may well still ask what the relevance of a religious figure like Jesus is for us in a scientifically oriented, democratic society, which puts great value on individual freedom. Indeed, what is the relevance of any ancient religious authority to our postmodern socio-psychological paradigm and practice of peacebuilding? Within this broader setting we now direct our attention to the significance of Jesus for modern justice and peacemaking.

The Jesus Factor in Justice *and* Peacemaking

Chapter 1

WHY NOT THE BIBLE?

The Holocaust and then more recently the dismantling of apartheid in South Africa have again raised questions of the possibility and appropriateness of political forgiveness, reconciliation, and reparations. Simon Wiesenthal's *The Sunflower: On the Possibilities and Limits of Forgiveness* raised a wide-ranging discussion about the appropriateness of forgiving the Nazi SS guards. And Desmond Tutu's *No Future Without Forgiveness* has given rise to a spirited debate about the justice of the process adopted by the Truth and Reconciliation Commission under his leadership.

Whether the debaters are aware of it or not, the concepts of forgiveness, reconciliation, and restorative justice stem directly from the teachings and example of Jesus and the prophetic tradition that preceded him. Unfortunately, however, the intramural debate among Christians themselves about the political significance of Jesus diminishes its effect. Jesus is being used to justify a wide variety of contradictory views of peace and peacemaking. Evangelical interpretation of Jesus as peacemaker ranges from televangelists who deride Islam and use Jesus' name to hasten the violence of Armageddon to those who in his name call for nonviolence and social justice.

Nevertheless, whether or not one is religiously inclined, the present socio-political climate in the United States is so infused with religious agitation that to be uninformed about the historical reality of Jesus and the genuine issues he raises impoverishes the dialogue. The issues are not only intramural but intercultural between Christianity, Islam, Hinduism, and Buddhism, not to mention secular civil religion. For peacemakers who claim to be Jesus' followers, the stakes are especially high.

But one may still raise the question why Jesus? Why not an appeal to the broader biblical tradition, or to the historical experience and theology of the Christian church? In answer to the first question it is precisely the interpretation of the biblical tradition that is at issue in an appeal to Jesus. Generalizing perhaps too broadly, the Hebrew tradition of peacekeeping recommended a fair, impartial retribution mitigated by compassion. Shalom (peace) in a just orderly society was to be maintained by a strictly limited legal formula of retaliation, namely, the *lex talionis* tempered by mercy. Forgiveness played a humanizing role in peacemaking, and it was urged as a pragmatic, moral alternative to vengeance. It was institutionalized in public rituals of atonement, but ultimately the concepts of justice and virtue required a retributive payment. The Jesus factor challenges precisely this notion of ultimate retaliatory retribution.

As for an appeal to the experience and theology of the church in history, it is abundantly evident that Christianity has and does condone violence as a means to peace. As John Macquarrie observed in his Firth lectures,

> Catholic popes and bishops have marched at the head of armies, Protestant reformers have led revolts and tyrannized over cities, churchmen of all sorts have entreated God to grant victory to the armies of their respective nations. Whether any of them ought to have done these things is, of course, another question.[2]

The history of the church is fraught with ambiguity, tension, and debate. As Gerald Schlabach notes in his study of Saint Augustine's theology, without Jesus' own voice as the Gospels ever communicate it to the church, the conversation will only mimic other conversations and may in fact teach Christians to turn elsewhere for ethical guidance.[3]

"Jesus' own voice," as Schlabach correctly states it, comes to us through the text of the Gospels, so an appeal to Jesus can not and should not dodge the biblical text. But our appeal is to the gospel *gestalt* of Jesus, that is, his full identity as God's messiah as portrayed in the New Testament and not merely to individual texts of the New Testament collated to form a theological ethic. This gestalt furnished by those who knew him best provides the perspective for reading the varying texts of the New Testament as well as the Old. Thus our appeal is to Jesus as he is presented to us in the historical documents, and not to the various and sometimes conflicting texts of the New Testament writings about peace and violence.

Through the manipulation of texts Jesus has too often been removed from his own cultural context in late antiquity and grossly misrepresented as teaching that peace is an interiorized (personalized) individual virtue which is consistent with a social-political philosophy of peace through violent political power. The challenge in considering the "Jesus factor" in justice and peacemaking is to allow him to emerge from his own culture with its idiosyncrasies and speak to our modern world.

Authority vs. Experience

But to introduce the Jesus factor into peacemaking raises the further question why we should insist on a religious reference at all, especially one that from the beginning has caused conflict. Ideas about the relevance of religion to peacemaking range all the way from the claims of Christopher Hitchens, who in his *God Is Not Great* argues that religion inclines people to violence and blind submission to authority and is therefore a major part of the problem, to those who claim that true peace is a spiritual condition and impossible apart from a correct doctrinal view and personal relationship to Jesus. The latter position is widely disseminated with the bumper sticker slogan, "No Jesus, no peace. Know Jesus, know peace!"

An appeal to religious authority suggests that we begin with the words of Holy Scripture and adapt our experience-based knowledge to their instructions. Put bluntly, it raises the question of the relevance of a divine dictate to democratically derived decisions. Thus to introduce the Jesus factor creates a methodological tension. The tension is felt most keenly in professional peacemaking disciplines with their empirically based vocabulary and techniques. Conflict transformation and restorative justice programs, for example, are practice-oriented and use tested methodologies. The appeal to Jesus points to an ancient non-empirical norm that in turn appeals to the will and power of God as the authority for healing human relationships and gives very little practical instruction. How are we to integrate the authority model and the empirical model based on psychological and sociological research and experience?

Some claim that the only way to truly honor "biblical" authority is to maintain a literal transfer of biblical language and moral precepts across cultures. We have a good example of this kind of thinking in the field of communication and human relations in some theological training programs. For example, in an attempt to bolster scriptural authority in the area of pastoral counseling, Southern Baptist Theological Seminary has changed the name of the department to "Biblical Counseling."[4] This approach insists that pastoral counseling take the form of literal biblical exhortation, which the counselor thinks applies to the case.

Applying this literalist model to peacebuilding would suggest a much more restricted use of biblical directives. Jesus' wisdom for resolving conflict as reported in Matthew 18:15-20, for example, would by implication become a formulaic prescription for church members with only doubtful relevance to broader peacemaking principles. As it stands, it is a marvelous insight into the dynamics of peacemaking.

I am persuaded that we need not be caught in the dilemma of choosing between religious authority and science based on empirical experience as defined by Hitchens and others. There is an alternative to this approach that recognizes the normativeness of Jesus, which Christians speak of as the "lordship of Christ," while at the same time recognizing the validity and usefulness of professional experience and research in the field of human relationships. As our modern culture shifts into its "postmodern," thoroughgoing empirical phase, we are not forced into a choice between literal imitation and a secularistic approach that rejects the value of religious wisdom.

In every generation the Scripture has of necessity been read through changing lenses as empirical information, developing technology, and social-cultural patterns have changed. Essential to the Christian view of Jesus as the embodiment of God's Word is the recognition that he is a *historical* figure clothed in the garb of an ancient Near Eastern culture which must be adapted to cultural change to remain relevant. It is the genius of the biblical record itself that this adaptation to changing cultural settings is recognized in its pages. Inasmuch as Christians claim that Jesus was a human being caught up in the web of history, such adaptation and contextualization is not only inevitable but necessary.

This does not mean leaving Jesus behind or forsaking his authority. Rather, recognizing the spirit of his historical example and teaching, we attempt to identify analogous modern situations where his words and example speak with authority in the changing cultures.

Indeed this has been the genius of Christian missionary expansion. The text of its Scriptures has been viewed as translatable and adaptable, which has enabled it to cross the various cultures of the globe! Thus we continue to take Jesus with utmost seriousness and find ways to implement his mission in all the varying cultures of humankind.

FROM APHORISM TO PRACTICE

Complicating the task of historical adaptation is the problem of Jesus' style of teaching. He speaks in the aphorisms and parables of a wisdom teacher, leaving only the most general kind of ethical rules. And as we have noted in the introduction, he clearly does not submit a legislative program that can form a political base. How shall we move from such parabolic sayings based on a profoundly religious presupposition to a legislator's guide based on political polls, or a practitioner's manual for modern mediators and peace builders? What can students in the disciplines of peace building find in the study of Jesus' life and teachings that will enhance their skills of mediation and conflict transformation? What, for example, might it add to the practical insights of authors like John Winslade and Gerald Monk in their book on narrative mediation,[5] which approaches conflict resolution from the philosophical perspective of social constructionism? Might they expect to find functional guidelines, formulas, or ethical imperatives?

Perhaps an example of the difficulty will help. It is generally agreed that forgiveness is at the heart of Jesus' teaching and example. But in conflict transformation how shall we apply his command to forgive without limits? Experience has demonstrated that in some cases unlimited forgiveness only encourages continuing abuse. Are there times and situations when in the spirit of Jesus one should not forgive? How far dare we qualify Jesus' teaching to fit the findings of empirical psychology and socio-political experience? Might a balance of forgiveness and retribution be more effective in the trauma healing process? Dare we use rational analysis in applying the aphorisms and parables to actual cases? Of course such questions assume that we already know what Jesus teaches about forgiveness, and we may be surprised to see how nuanced his words are. How is the authority model to be integrated into the empirical professional model?[6]

JESUS' NEW PARADIGM

What is it about Jesus that has caused the church to call him "Son of God" and makes him essential to the Christian style of peacemaking? How can we explain to those of other faiths what it is about him that still challenges us to follow him as the "pioneer of our faith?" That, of course, is the theme of the whole book, but in brief, if we cannot expect to gain new techniques and functional guidelines, what may we reasonably anticipate from an exploration of his life and teachings? Do we expect only inspiration and spiritual encouragement to live by a moral ideal? Shall we look for an ideal saintly model? Shall we look for a Jesus style of peacemaking? Or does religious experience only furnish the nurturing backdrop and motivation for learning professional peace making disciplines?

I suggest first that it is Jesus' "style" that sets him apart from founders and representatives of other major religions. For example, although Gandhi virtually identified the teachings of Krishna and Christ, Lord Krishna's advice to Arjuna on the field of battle suggests a style and pattern of action quite different from Jesus. Krishna justifies the use of military violence and suggests that for Arjuna not to advance in battle against the enemy is an act of weakness and cowardice. He justifies necessary and unavoidable violence by reminding Arjuna that the soul "is not slain when the body is slain." Therefore Arjuna should obey Lord Krishna's command and attack his kinsmen in a spirit of saintly obedience, not out of anger or revenge.

By contrast Jesus' style is most clearly depicted in the theme of cross and resurrection. Facing execution and the defeat of his nascent movement, he refused the option of violent resistance. The cross, which is the symbol of his execution and defeat, became the identifying symbol of his ongoing movement. And as John H. Yoder has somewhere pointed out, taking up the cross is the only direct command that Jesus gave to all those who would follow him. It is precisely what Reinhold Niebuhr called the "impossible possibility" of his challenge that makes him both the provocative stimulus and the despair of peacemakers.

Jesus represents what we refer to as a paradigm change in framing the goals and methods of peacemaking. He does not give us a lot of new information or change all the rules for social behavior. Indeed, much of his teaching reinforces an implicit nonviolent substratum of the Hebrew prophets. Neither does he give us much practical political advice or new psychological analysis of conflict and its consequences. *But he does provide a basic pattern or framework of spiritual assumptions, and moral perspectives within which to work at approaches and strategies to modern peacemaking.*

This new paradigm begins with the basic theistic assumption of the Hebrew Scriptures, namely, that Yahweh, the God of Israel, is creator and sustainer of the universe. God has created human beings in the divine image thus endowing them with moral dignity and responsibility for themselves and the earth and has fixed the moral boundaries for social intercourse. Thus humankind is accountable to a transcendent Source, God, for the mutual well-being of each other in community. This responsibility includes the authority to regulate the social order according to their understanding of God's laws.

Jesus' basic world view and theological assumptions remained Hebraic, but he differed with contemporary rabbinic implication and practice. His agreement is implied in his full approval of the Jewish lawyer's summary of the law as love for God with all one's being and love of the neighbor as oneself. In reply to the lawyer's question, "What shall I do to inherit eternal life?" Jesus only replied that his summary was right, and that he should do what the law requires. "Do this," he said, "and you will live" (Luke 10: 25-28). What changed the paradigm was Jesus' understanding of God, and his definition of the neighbor.

The change is first in Jesus' view of God's impartiality and universal availability irrespective of humankind's cultural religious identity. Impartiality as a rule for judging fairly was firmly established in Israel's culture as a characteristic of Yahweh, but they made no secret of God's partiality toward Israel as a nation. There were prophets like Amos who challenged the idea that God had favorites, but Jesus as he was understood by his immediate followers went beyond this. For him the Jewish religion, symbolized in the Mosaic Law and Jerusalem temple, was not the funnel through which all must enter God's kingdom. God has no favorites among the peoples/cultures of the world but responds to the sincere compliance from the heart to God's law of the universe—*wisdom*—which Jewish wisdom literature associated with the Torah.[7]

In his writings Paul emphasizes God's impartiality in accepting all humankind, "Jew or Gentile" (Rom 2:11), and this emphasis clearly comes from his life-changing revelation of Jesus. Paul's insistence on humble openness (faith) to God as the only way to reconciliation and peace echoes Jesus' ready acceptance and even praise of the non-Jewish individuals who approached him in faith. This does not change the moral and spiritual boundaries for peacemakers, but it does discredit claims to religious imperialism in the name of monotheistic faith. Religious mantras, doctrines, rites, and ceremonies are not essential to the peace of God, but rather genuine transformation, what Paul in Galatians 6:15-16 calls "a new creation." Or again, as Paul puts it, it is "only faith working through love" that counts (Gal 5:6). In this he is clearly faithful to the message of Jesus.

Second, while Jesus' understanding of peace remained the Hebrew shalom—neighbors living in peace and social well-being under God's covenant—the new paradigm defines *neighbor to include enemy*. The different lines of obligation to friend and enemy, to neighbor or stranger, "Jew or Gentile" are erased. According to the parable of the Good Samaritan, which follows Jesus' conversation with the lawyer, "neighbor" does not define the other person who has the correct address, class, ethnic, or racial characteristics, but the one who acts as neighbor toward the other. The Levitical laws called for treating a resident alien as a citizen (19: 33-34), but Jesus levels the field of moral responsibility between neighbor and alien. "Neighbor" defines the one in need.

The question is not whether he or she (third person) is my neighbor, but whether I (first person) am willing to be neighbor to another in need. So Jesus commands, "Love your enemies and pray for them that persecute you" (Matt. 5:43-44). It is this redefinition of the enemy as neighbor that reframes the prohibition on all retaliation.

The definition of love (*agape*) for the other remains compassion, empathy, and respect, and the test of love's sincerity is whether it is the kind of love we have for ourselves, i.e., the attitude or stance one has toward oneself. We are to love our neighbor/enemy as we love ourselves (Matt. 22: 37-39). C. S. Lewis once pointed out in a sermon on forgiveness that this love for ourselves is not "feelings of fondness or affection," approval or indulgence, thinking bad people are nice, or approving other persons when their behavior is clearly unfair or injurious.[8] Rather, it is our self-love that allows us to "forgive ourselves 'seventy times seven'" even when we strongly disapprove what we have done! Love is the good will that makes it possible to separate the evil deed from the person doing the deed and seek the person's redemption.

It is this subtle but radical changing of the paradigm plus his self-sacrifice and total dependence on God for his own vindication that caused Jesus' followers to identify him as the embodiment of the divine light that through the ages has overcome darkness and sustained the shalom of the human community (John 1:1-14). And he called his followers to continue his mission by being light and salt in human society (Matt. 5:13-14). It was this that led his followers to the conviction that he is, in the words of John A. T. Robinson's book title, "the human face of God" for us.

A Postscript to Evangelicals: Which Jesus?

Is this normative claim for Jesus relevant in a pluralistic democracy where a humanistic assumption forms the only common base? Unfortunately evangelical ideology, which is most focused on Jesus as God's peacemaker, has become the unaware abettor of his irrelevance to the social/political process of peacemaking.

Surely the answer to this question is implicit in the question itself. The most orthodox definition of Jesus' identity speaks of him as not only fully divine but also fully human. Indeed, his divinity is not a separate individualized part of his identity but an essential part of and revealed through his humanity. It is as "son of man" that he is disclosed as "Son of God." A large part of modern evangelical theology's difficulty in relating to the political scene stems from its implicit reductionism of the christological reality in its own tradition.

It has failed to explore the implications of its own christological definition of Jesus as fully human. Jesus is reduced to a God-figure focused only on spiritual salvation which has little to do with a just human society—what in Hebrew is called shalom.

If Jesus is to be relevant to political peacebuilding, he must be understood as a fully human being in the historical setting of his own ancient Jewish culture. He cannot be introduced as the *deus ex machina* of ancient Greek and Roman dramas, that is, a miraculous divinity arrived to resolve the apparently irresolvable human dilemma. He must be seen as a fully historical individual immersed in and struggling with the complexities of violent human society.

Anything less than this suggests a contrived solution and an implicitly deistic view of as God aloof from the human scene or at best interrupting the human process with overwhelming power. We need to see Jesus not only as the "God-Man"—the true paradigm for understanding God, but as "God's man"—the true paradigm for humanity. Viewed in this way, new perspectives on his relevance for political peacebuilding come into the picture.

On the one hand, Jesus' nonviolent peace mandates should not be viewed either as political pragmatism (a danger of liberal pacifism), or dismissed as politically irrelevant eschatological promises for some future time (the danger of evangelical realism). They represent rather a realistic understanding of the essential nature of human community as intended by God; and they represent, as we said earlier, a consistently nonviolent, but not necessarily non-coercive, way to transform conflict in human society. They are valid even though they do not "work" as an immediate pragmatic solution to every conflict. They are the way to work at the ongoing intractable conflicts caused by human selfishness, greed, and anger. They assume not the efficacy of human ingenuity but the faithfulness of God to the word spoken in Jesus.

Thus the first theological task is not to construct a creedal rationale based on traditional or Anabaptist orthodoxy to guide political peacemaking. Rather, the first task is to understand the original life pattern, the Jesus gestalt, that gives rise to and validates the very idea of nonviolent peacemaking in a violent world. In short, what is the Jesus pattern as reported/witnessed in the New Testament, which underlies the essential concept? What are its cultural and religious presuppositions? What is its social style or pattern? What kind of vocabulary does it use? This same stimulus/impulse drove the sixteenth-century Anabaptists to go back to the sources for guidance amid the cultural revolution known as the Protestant Reformation.

Chapter Two

JESUS AND RELIGIOUS PLURALISM

Religions are cultural creations. They are the human response to what is understood to be a disclosure of the great Mystery that surrounds us. They embody the "word" and "vision" that have been conveyed and form the basis for cultural and national identities. Allah is Islam's deity, and Muslims are the people of Allah. Yahweh is Judaism's deity, and Israel is the people of Yahweh. In like manner Shiva, Krishna, and Vishnu are Hindu deities; and the Trinity disclosed in Jesus defines Christian identity.

All too easily this self-identification of deity and nation becomes a possessive religious identity and in turn becomes competitive. Too often religious institutions operate at the childish level of "My daddy is greater than your daddy!" Our exclusive truth claims become the fodder for conflict rather than disclosure of the greater truth that lies beyond us all. We forget that in reality there can be and is only one Ultimate, and in the words of Paul, this Ultimate is "the Father from whom every family in heaven and on earth takes its name" (Eph. 3:14).

In the following two chapters we will examine the nature of this conflict that complicates peacebuilding and explore the question of Jesus' perspective on the religious pluralism of his day. Do the imperialistic and competitive messianic claims made for him in the intervening centuries reflect his own self-understanding? Was his approach to "Gentiles," that is, people of non-Jewish religions and cultures, unequivocally nonviolent? Or was his *non*violence implicitly based on the premise of a Jewish God's ultimate *violent* vindication of his life and mission? Violence delayed in the vindication of right is not nonviolence.

CHRISTIANITY AMONG WORLD RELIGIONS

At the present writing, religious and cultural fundamentalisms are fomenting violence in the Middle East, Asia, Africa, and more. And modern Christian and Judaic fundamentalist claims have only exacerbated the conflict. So to state the religious question as "the Jesus factor" seems on its face to raise the question, if not the claim, of religious exclusiveness—and such claims relying on competition and violent resolution directly challenge the goals and methods of mediation, conflict transformation and reconciliation. By its nature peacebuilding necessitates dialogue, listening, confession, and collaboration. It does not call for the erasure of all cultural-religious differences, but it does require the collaborative efforts of all involved. Exclusive religious claims and refusal to learn in dialogical conversation contradict the very methodology and goals of peacemaking.

Fundamentalist claims, no matter in which religious tradition they occur, cripple the peace process. This is especially problematic for monotheistic religions like Judaism, Islam, and Christianity which make very high claims for their human founders and their sacred books, but it is also true of religions like Hinduism, which pride themselves on their tolerance and inclusiveness.

Thus the modern Christian fundamentalist claim that Jesus is the exclusive way to genuine peace has become an embarrassment to many in the Christian peace movements. This embarrassment is heightened by Christianity's involvement in violent competition and domination through the centuries, and raises the question, despite Christian assertions, whether Jesus has any special claim to relevance for resolving conflicts among cultures and nations. Even many of those who acknowledge Jesus as the source and dynamic of their programs hesitate to explicitly speak his name or articulate the distinctive features of his approach to peacemaking for fear of sounding fundamentalistic.

The church claims that Jesus bears a special relation to Deity as "God's Son" and thus is the final word of God. This goes beyond the claims most other religions make for their founders. In comparison Buddha makes no claims to religious sainthood or exclusive truth. While Hinduism claims divinity for its leaders like Krishna and Siva, and has been plagued by its cultural and institutional fundamentalism, on the whole it has advocated syncretism and religious tolerance. Mohammed makes absolute truth claims for Koranic revelation, but for himself he claimed only the role of a prophet who recognized the authority of Moses and Jesus before him. Judaism honors Moses and the Torah but asserts no divine claims for him or the prophets who followed.

As one among other religions, therefore, Christianity's special claims heighten its obligation to clear its reputation of fundamentalistic exclusivism. Thus special importance attaches to the question whether Jesus himself was exclusivist in his approach and if so in what sense—a question to which the whole of this essay is tangentially addressed.

Each of the major religions has its own definition and approach to peace. In the Buddhist tradition peace is an inward serenity achieved through self-control, disciplined desire, and a nonviolent lifestyle. It can be attained by the realization of the "Four Noble Truths" and following the Eightfold Path. Islam, as the name implies, believes that peace is achieved through submission to the will of God as spelled out in the system of laws and practices revealed in the Koran through the Prophet Mohammed.

Combining ideas from Hinduism and Christianity, Gandhi held that nonviolence and truth are at the heart of peace and justice. Classical Hebraic tradition based peace on the covenant law established with Israel through Moses. Shalom (peace) was understood as the social order of justice, compassion, and obedience to the religious laws of Yahweh. While each of these traditions share overlapping values, each with its distinctive cultural definitions relates to conflict transformation from a different perspective.

Christianity as an institutional religion is one of these comparative religions and must justify itself not on its theological claims to superiority but on its historical record. Emerging out of Judaism in the first century CE, it shares Judaism's basic history and values, and must be classed with these other religions as a cultural construct. Its world view, theological rationale, and ethical systems are a combination of cultural values and the religious insight stemming from Jesus whom it accepts as the Messiah, or special representative, of God. It bases its claims of universal validity on special revelation and claims superiority for its truth as do its kindred religions, Islam, and Judaism. Nevertheless it shares many of the values and human weaknesses of other major religions.

Thus as one religion among competitors, Christianity is obligated to demonstrate on the historical landscape the superiority (if it is indeed superior) of its concept of peace and peacebuilding. Rational theological arguments for its truth such as Fundamentalism advances are insufficient. Christianity must justify its claims in and through respectful dialogue and experimentation with other religions. Recognizing the universality of God's concern for and self-disclosure to humankind, it must submit itself to the discipline of contextualizing the claim of its own sacred Scriptures, that Jesus was *the historical embodiment of God's peace for all humankind*. Thus it must be willing to ask again and again how Jesus, whom the church makes normative for peacemaking in our world, relates to the global cacophony of religious answers.

JESUS AND RELIGION

The nature of his claims and their implications for those of other religious cultures is an intensely debated issue in scholarly circles. While this is not the place to enter into the often contentious debate that has divided the theological world of Christendom, we do need to be clear about how we read the Gospels as a basis for peacemaking in our multireligious global context. Jesus' words and example can be read in different ways, and would-be peacemakers cannot avoid taking a position.

We need to ask whether the church's messianic claims for Jesus inevitably carry exclusivistic implications in the ideological battle between religions. How, indeed, is Jesus related to the "culture wars?" And what is the nature of "peace on earth among people of good will," which the angels announced at his birth? I would argue that Jesus' claims are not exclusivist—but inclusive by virtue of his uncompromised nonviolent character. His social concept of peace is an integral part of his faith convictions. His perspective is explicitly religious. For him peace, or shalom, is the peace of Yahweh, the God of Israel, who is God of the universe. But this does not necessarily imply that he is the founder of a new religion of which he himself is the warrior leader in a worldwide crusade.

If we are to take seriously his nonviolent cross as God's peace strategy, we must consider seriously its implications for the reconciliation of conflicting cultural religions. The crusades, whether medieval or modern with their imperialistic goals based ultimately on the threat of God's violence, need to end. New paradigms of peace and peacemaking modeled on the example of Jesus as God's man for us must be framed.

Christian orthodoxy has traditionally insisted that Jesus' earthly mission was exclusively to Israel, and his messianic calling was to initiate a new religion emerging out of and supplanting Judaism as the true religion. This reading leaves us with a kind of religious fundamentalism presumably established by Jesus himself. Peace, then, is defined as a spiritual rapprochement—"peace with God," and is brought about by satisfying the retributive justice of God's law. This peace with God is spread by converting individuals to the new religious image of Jesus as personal savior.

In this manner Jesus becomes the exclusive mediator of peace between God and individuals and thus the only valid arbiter of peace between conflicting human societies. The bumper sticker sound bite, "No Jesus, no peace: Know Jesus, know peace" encapsulates this peace message. Jesus' words in John 14: 6, "I am the way, the truth and the life" are interpreted as an exclusive religious claim and used to validate this view.

While this has been the dominant view of orthodoxy, it is not the only Christian reading of the New Testament story. Two currents flow through the history of Israel as it is reported in the Bible. The vision of nationalistic Israel, which understands its messianic calling to be the imperialistic agent of Yahweh establishing his exclusive authority over the whole earth, is the dominant one. This is the stream of thought that lionizes the accomplishments of David and his son Solomon. The other current is that of Israel as God's nonviolent messianic servant. Needless to say, the nationalistic stream represents a more exclusivist position. But the picture of Jesus as the Messiah represents the nonviolent stream of the "suffering Servant." Within this stream there is a generous inclusiveness that is not threatened by God's acceptance of the foreigner.

Those Christians who hold to a retributive interpretation of Christ's execution on the cross insist most vehemently on the exclusivist claims of Christianity, but as James Orr, the great evangelical theologian, pointed out over a century ago, this theory has never been made formal church dogma. The crucifixion of Jesus can and must be viewed as the outrage of human depravity against the genuine nonviolent goodness of God manifest in his life. His resurrection, then, is understood as God's vindication of Jesus' example of nonviolent servanthood, and justification of all those who commit themselves to him to follow his way of life regardless of their cultural identity and religious affiliation. Thus, as the writer to the Hebrews puts it, Jesus became the "pioneer and perfecter of our faith" (12:2) who reconciles us to God.

While John's Gospel clearly exalts Jesus as the embodiment of humanity's only way to salvation, i.e., to "the Father's house" (14:2), we need not read this in exclusivist terms. According to John 1:1-14, Jesus is the dynamic "word" spoken in the creation, and the universal "light" that has shown forth in the darkness from the beginning. And it is this eternal Word that John claims is the Father's human embodiment of the way for humanity to come home to God. Indeed, he can represent Jesus as saying, "If you know me, you will know the Father also" (v. 7), and "I am in the Father and the Father in me" (v. 11).

Indeed the course of self-sacrificial love and nonviolence as embodied in Jesus is the only way humankind can fulfill its God-intended destiny of shalom. Read in this way, Jesus' claim does not exclude any of those who have found "the Father's" true and living way, regardless of their culture and religion.

JESUS AND TEMPLE JUDAISM

Jesus was, of course, a Jew from Galilee and identified himself with Israel and Jewish culture. But Judaism was a national cultural collective with a wide variety of classes and ethnic groups. Thus to more precisely understand the implications of the messianic claims for Jesus and his perspective on non-Jewish religions one must consider his relation to the Jerusalem temple and its cult.

Jesus clearly conceived the nation of Israel as the focus of his mission, and within Judaism the messianic role or vocation was clearly defined. The Messiah was to first purify the Hebrew religion and liberate the nation of Israel. Then as king of the Jewish religious state he would spread the dominion of Judaism. But, and this is the significant thing, *Jesus redefined the meaning of the messianic role.* Instead of defining the religion of Israel as the only right religion and proselyting the nations, he invited Israel to become the vanguard of peacemaking among the nations through sacrificial self-giving.

The Gospel stories indicate this more open and generous messianic stance of Jesus toward people of other cultural faiths in a number of ways. Matthew, for example, notes that eastern astrologers were alerted to Jesus' birth by an astrological omen in their own religious idiom. As Michael Molnar has pointed out, these "signs" were not miraculous spectacles seen by everyone in the Middle East.[9] They were signs that astrologers acquainted with the Greek zodiac and astral divinations would recognize.

The significant implications of this are seldom noted, but Zoroastrian astrologers recognized him as the kingly fulfillment of messianic traditions not by studying the Hebrew Scriptures but taking into account the Greek zodiac. Clearly the writer of Matthew recognizes this as authentic enlightenment and includes these Magi in the circle of the saved community.

In Luke's Gospel the angels announce peace on earth *to all people of good will* as a consequence of his birth. Again, the phrase "all people of good will" indicates an audience much broader than "those who accept Christian orthodoxy." Although a king (Messiah), "the son of David," he is born in the most humble circumstances. *His birth does not presage peace through hegemonic religious domination but through God's offer of conflict transformation across religious boundaries*!

When Jesus healed the Roman centurion's servant and the Phoenician mother's child, he did not demand conversion as a condition. And while these stories are presented as exceptions to his main ministry directed to Israel, the universal implications of his messianic vocation are clear.

John's Gospel uses Jesus' meeting with a woman of the despised Samaritan sect as the setting for his announcement that true spiritual worship of "the Father" defies sacred tradition and boundaries (4:23-24)! While Jesus affirms that the God who revealed himself as "Father" through Hebrew and Jewish history is the true God, this true God is not confined to the Jewish religion. John uses this Samaritan setting for Jesus to announce that he is indeed the Messiah whose message will cross religious and cultural boundaries.

Again in John's Gospel Jesus announces that he has "other sheep" not of the Jewish-Christian fold that will listen to his voice, and he must gather them into the sheepfold (John 10:16). Already during his earthly ministry such talk stirred up dissension and raised questions about the legitimacy of his messiahship just as it does today.

Both Mark and Matthew report an incident in which Jesus reproved his disciples when they laid exclusive claim to his "name." (Jesus' "name" indicates his spirit and character. See Mark 10:38-41.) His disciples rebuked a man who was casting out demons in Jesus' name because he was not part of their crowd. Jesus in turn rebuked his disciples saying, "Do not stop him; for no one who does a deed of power in my name will be able soon afterward to speak evil of me. Whoever is not against us is for us."

The question was not the exorcist's religious affiliation—but the authenticity of his claim to the "name" of Jesus, which was demonstrated in his casting out demons. Surely this test of authenticity is the crucial one for peacemaking inasmuch as casting out demons of trauma, resentment, and hostility is peacemakers' work!

But the most important indicator of Jesus' stance toward those of other cultures and religions was his attitude toward the Jewish temple and cultus. The Jewish temple represented the exclusive claims of Israel to be the messianic representative of God's peace among the nations. When Jesus "cleansed" the temple of the apparatus that identified it with Jewish cultural exclusivity, he declared that God's house was to be a "house of prayer for all people." Instead of enhancing the exclusive religious superiority of the Jewish temple, he opened it to all nations as the house of prayer. Thus he clearly distinguished his own messianic mission of peacemaking from the hegemonic expectations of first-century Judaism.

Jesus was understood to say that he would destroy the old temple and in three days build another one not made with hands (Mark 14:58). While his words were misused at his trial to indicate an anti-Jewish bias, his disciples understood them to mean that his death and resurrection would raise a new meeting place of God and humans (a "temple") that was not restricted to the locus and forms of the Jewish religion. Stephen, the first martyr of the new movement, was also accused of blaspheming the temple and saying that "Jesus of Nazareth will destroy this place and will change the customs that Moses handed on to us" (Acts 6: 13-14).

Insofar as the temple symbolized the exclusive prerogatives of the Jewish religion, it represented a barrier to the messianic peace Jesus preached, and the Jesus movement did threaten its preeminence. But as Paul indicates, Jesus did not organize a new religion to take the preeminent place of Judaism. Rather he broke down the walls of hostility between competing religious and cultural groups (Eph. 2:14) and leveled the playing field for participation in God's rule of peace (what Jesus referred to as "the kingdom of God").

THE JESUS PARADIGM AND GLOBAL CULTURES

Between the Jesus of the Gospels and today's global religious scene lie two millenia of exclusive claims in the name of Jesus—crusades, pogroms, church schisms, religious wars, invasions of "heathen" territories under the banner of the cross, all of which still raise suspicions and conflict. Such exclusive claims have almost inevitably been related to the self-serving ambitions of ecclesial and nationalistic institutions, and the peace achieved in the name of these claims has been based on violence in contradiction to the spirit of Jesus. Whether caused by well-intended misunderstanding of Jesus' own claims or by religio-political imperialism that manipulates Jesus' message to justify the goals of Christendom, this long history hampers Christian efforts for peace.

But despite this historical development, the Jesus paradigm has continued to function as a nonviolent factor working for shalom. The significance of this influence is typified in the reverence for men like Saint Francis of Assisi in our Western Christian culture. And the power of its ongoing effect is seen in the many Christian NGOs at work among the impoverished majorities of the world. Its power of influence in other world cultures is typified in figures like Mahatma Gandhi, who readily admitted Jesus' influence. In any case it is important to examine briefly the nature of such monarchial claims and the reason for their persistence in the Christian world.

We need to remember that the claims for Jesus' messianic mission were made in the context of Jewish expectations that the Messiah would establish the authoritative administrative control, that is, the hegemonic domination, of the Jewish religion.[10] The Messiah would come and rule from the temple in Jerusalem converting all nations, bringing them into submission to Israel's God and thus establish shalom. But Jesus turned this expectation of religious dominion on its head! The "kingdom" that he offered was not ruled over by a just and beneficent dictator but by a heavenly Father who offered his blessings to humanity seemingly indiscriminate of culture and religion.

The message of the first followers of Jesus also inherently challenged the competitive imperialism of Judaic monotheism and offered a non-competitive, nonviolent "faith" that transcended claims of all cultural religions. The old "walls" of culture religion, even the Jewish religion, were breached, and a new cross-cultural shalom was offered without national distinctions and special privileges. That was the implication of monotheism in the original Christian movement. Thus teachers like the apostle Paul downplayed the significance of Jewish rituals and taboos that excluded "Gentiles" and in their place elevated faith that comprehended the true meaning of Jesus and his mission.[11]

Unfortunately this Jesus paradigm changed character over the early centuries as it crossed cultural landscapes. Instead of continuing to focus on the Divine Mystery disclosed in the *character* of Jesus and the rule of God that he embodied, Christianity adopted the rational philosophical metaphors and technical vocabulary of the Greco-Roman world to formulate its "orthodoxy."

Monotheism was defined not as belief in the one "Father from whom every family in heaven and on earth takes its name" who is accessible universally through faith, but as the only rational definition of ultimate Transcendent Being (Greek, *to On*). And the authentic God-reality in Jesus was defined as a divine *ontological substance*—"of one substance with the Father." Thus the Jewish Messiah became a divinity after the image of Roman divinities in contrast to the messianic son of God. He became a "god" superior to all others and in cultural competition with them.

In the New Testament Jesus' deity is defined in terms of his intimate relationship to God rather than in terms of his divine substance as one of the Trinity. His is a family relationship and likeness—"like father like son." In character and relationship his disciples experienced him as the authentic word of God, the truth and light that all through the centuries had shown in the darkness—the embodiment of God among us. His God-identity was known through a personal social identity of relationship that bridged the gap between God and humanity. And as we have seen, this God relationship came through as a generous, welcoming, noncompetitive relationship showering the blessings of sunshine and rain impartially on every human being, yet, as we shall see later, without indulgence, cooperation with evil, or deceit.[12]

By contrast, the metaphysical paradigm, which the church of the third and fourth century adopted, was based on the metaphor of physical material substance. This church conceived of spirit as material substance highly refined, but substance nonetheless. Thus to accent essence or reality, the church spoke of the gods in terms of substantial spiritual being. Based on this kind of metaphor, the church theologians insisted on defining Jesus' deity in terms of exclusive God-substance, which infinitely distinguished and set him apart from every other cultural conceptualization of God. In the words of John Keenan, "It is these patterns—with their implicit assumptions and explicit tenets—that prove troublesome in contemporary attempts to enunciate the meaning of Christ in the context of our world."[13]

This theological spin was a subtle but crucial shift that changed how the church's claims for Jesus as "Son of God" were understood. With the passing of centuries, the strictly voluntary religious Christian minority became Christendom, which Alan Kreider describes as "a symbiosis of religious and state authorities, [with] the ultimate sanction of force," and Jesus as second person of the Trinity became the exclusive God of Christendom.[14] "Pagans," which originally meant "country dwellers," became "heathen" whose gods were idols in violent competition with Christ.

Christian Orthodoxy's exclusive claims for its religious system evolved in this manner. Inevitably such exclusive claims place it in competition with the cultural conceptions of all other religious paradigms. Peace becomes toleration based on a balance of power rather than a genuine shalom of nonviolent relationships. What we need to do, then, is to put the distinctive claims for Jesus made in the New Testament back into the context of their ancient cultural situation and to understand them in terms that make dialogue and cooperation possible with those who bring other cultural perspectives to the peacemaking table

RE-SCRIBING THE EXCLUSIVE PARADIGM

Scholars from Adolph Harnack and Albert Schweitzer at the beginning of the twentieth century to the current Jesus Seminar have attempted to discover the true "historical Jesus" and relate him to the present scene. That is not my intent. Rather, because the essential nature of God's peace mission is at issue, I want to suggest a way of reading the New Testament materials that frames the deity of Jesus, the Messiah, differently from the exclusive terms of fourth-century Hellenized Christianity and Nicaean Orthodoxy

There can be little doubt that the gospel writers viewed Jesus as the messianic "Son of God," and that the first-century church hailed him as "Lord"—a term reserved for Yahweh in Hebrew religion. But the word *Lord* (*kurios* in the Greek) was also ascribed to the emperor Caesar, who considered himself to be the manifestation of God in human form. Thus, not the term itself but the form of divine lordship was at issue. Was Jesus a "Lord" *like* Caesar? Or, in the words of John's Gospel, was his kingdom not like worldly kingdoms? In the ancient Graeco-Roman setting the church councils defined Jesus' deity as an exclusive divine power broker like Caesar.

The question we must ask is what convinced Jesus' followers that he was truly the human embodiment of God's word, as John puts it (John 1:14)? How did they describe the astonishing God-reality that they experienced in him? And how might this change the traditional exclusivism of Christian orthodoxy in its approach to people of other faiths? Is it an exclusive essence that separates him and those who follow his religion from all other cultural religions? Or is it an inclusive image that all human cultures potentially share as creatures created in God's image?

There can be no doubt that the New Testament Gospels are concerned to articulate the *unique God-reality* in Jesus, but they base it on character and action, not essence. The Gospel of John, which is the most Greek in it perspective, clearly represents this difference of approach. John opens his account of Jesus' ministry with the affirmation that he was the embodiment of the dynamic "Word" of God already working in the creation. Many years ago in his paraphrase of the Gospels, J. B. Phillips translated this "*Logos*" as "God spoke," indicating its dynamic character. The word was an effective deed. It is not a word of rational explanation or theological theory, but a creative act. And now, John says, this spoken word of grace and truth, which has prevailed on the human scene from the beginning, has been embodied in Jesus of Nazareth. The reality of Emmanuel ("God with us") present in Jesus is manifested in his deeds of transformation, which are inclusive by their very nature, and invite respect and communication even with enemies.

The synoptic Gospels substantiate this same God-claim but in a slightly different way. Each is a montage to be read as a holistic image made up of individual pictures. They are not intended to be biographical accounts of the founder of Christianity, as is often assumed, and they certainly do not define his divine essence or substance. Rather they form a whole gestalt, image, or impression of his messianic deity by depicting astonishing and often misunderstood actions and teachings. The reality of God-present is to be seen in his embodiment of the transforming effects of his acts.

Thus Jesus is presented as one who acts with God's authority. He forgives sins, heals diseases, challenges purity taboos, brings life out of death, and rebukes the injustice of racism and sexism—all introducing God's shalom. In short, he does the transforming works of God demonstrating the power and authority of God. When the imprisoned John Baptist sent to know whether he truly was the Messiah, Jesus replied, "Go tell John what you see me doing."

In the communicational currency of that day these works are described as miracles, that is, surprising, even "impossible," acts of God. Jesus not only heals all manner of physical and psychological diseases, he calms the wind and waves and walks on water. He sends demons into swine herds. What peacebuilders who claim to operate in his name must learn to do is translate these miracles into the modern idiom. And as every peacebuilder knows, the work of restoring shalom is indeed dependent on miracles! Like Peter they must walk on water confident only in the miraculous power of the Jesus factor. Dependence on such power makes people of all religious worldviews co-dependent on the transformative power of the God disclosed in Jesus.

Chapter 3

THE JESUS STYLE OF PEACEMAKING

In 1972 when John H. Yoder wrote his *Politics of Jesus*, the Billy Graham crusades were still at their height. Already Graham's *Peace with God: the Secret of Happiness*, written a decade before, had become a classic of American Evangelicalism. In both Yoder's and Graham's volumes Jesus' cross stands as an icon of peace, but peace and the process of peacemaking remain to be defined. Does his cross represent a change in our way of understanding God's approach to peacemaking? Or is Jesus' execution merely a bending to the inexorable demand of the universe for retributive justice? Are we simply looking for a shift in *strategies* to put Jesus' program of peacemaking into operation? Or does Jesus have a distinctive *style*? I believe that Jesus' style represents a theological paradigm shift that changes the perspective from which we understand peacemaking.

In Protestant Evangelicalism, Jesus' cross represents no change of *style*. Peace with God is not based on a new understanding of God's holiness but merely on God's relenting mercy toward those who will accept his gracious offer to satisfy his own demands. The law demanding retribution (*law of talion*) remains intact. Violent retribution remains the norm. The right to overlook offenses against divine holiness is based not on God's infinite goodness but on satisfying God's need for vindication before the natural law of the universe. Peace is understood as the assuaging of God's anger, and it is experienced as inner release from a burden of fear, guilt, and inadequacy to keep God's just commandments.

According to this paradigm, peace depends on the continuing use or ultimate threat of violence. In the words of Henry Wadsworth Longfellow's poem, "The Challenge of Thor,"

> Force rules the world still,
> Has ruled it, shall rule it;
> Meekness is weakness,
> Strength is triumphant,
> Over the whole earth
> Still is it Thor's Day!
> Thou art a God too,
> O Galilean!
> And thus single-handed
> Unto the combat,
> Gauntlet or Gospel,
> Here I defy thee!

Yoder's very title implicitly challenged the acceptance of the law of talion as the yardstick of vindication and the basis for peacemaking. It suggested that the cross of Jesus represents a *style* or pattern change in the moral basis for peacemaking. It suggests that not the law of talion but what has come to be referred to as the nonviolent "grain of the universe" provides the base for peacemaking. Here the cross itself is a symbol of a lifestyle, and following Jesus' example in "cross bearing" is an essential aspect of peacemaking. The nonviolent *politics*, that is, way of doing peacemaking in human society, involves us in "carrying a cross." It marks a turning away from the values of Roman *imperium* represented in the *Pax Romana* and the peace based on imperial military might and authority.

And so we ask the question, Does Jesus have a distinctive style? Or does he represent simply a change in strategy that redirects and radicalizes the goals of justice and peace as they were spelled out in the Hebrew Bible? In 2006 yet another book entitled, *The Politics of Jesus: Recovering the True Revolutionary Nature of Jesus' Teachings and How They Have Been Corrupted*, caused a flurry of discussion and debate. The author, Obery Hendricks, tries to explain how the revolutionary Jesus has been turned into the "meek and mild" Jesus of current American society and suggests eight "strategies" for social justice that will recapture the radical social message of Jesus. But Hendricks' approach raises the question whether the Jesus factor is one of "strategy" or "style."

I will argue that it is Jesus' distinctive perspective or style that distinguishes his way of peacemaking. He represents more than a shift in social strategy or a spiritual transmutation of moral values. In the following chapters we will examine the historical-cultural aspects of this style and how they might translate into our modern democratic society. But first an overview of Jesus' style.

Lord Jesus, Lord Buddha

Toward the close of the United States' war with Vietnam I was visiting Saigon (now Ho Chi Minh City). Christian missionaries who shared antiwar convictions with local Buddhist friends arranged a semi-private conversation between a respected monk and me on the subject of peace. We both objected to the violence that even as we spoke threatened the perimeters of the city.

We were there to compare the views of our respective religious communities and explore the possibilities for cooperative witness against the war. We were to discuss in fraternal fashion the similarities and differences of our traditions on the question of peace. Our awareness that neither Vietnamese nor American officials would approve our meeting heightened the intensity of the meeting.

Some time into the discussion I noticed that my Buddhist friend began each of his responses with the phrase, "Lord Buddha says." It was a gracious non-polemic recognition that the Buddha had taught a distinct way to achieve peace. Up to that point I had attempted to clarify the Christian approach to peace and peacemaking in irenic terms without direct reference to the "Lord Jesus." But through his responses I was made clearly aware that we represented two quite distinct traditions, and I too began to make direct reference to the Lord Jesus. I became conscious that before we could cooperate we needed, in Thich Nhat Hahn's words, to be "mindful" of each other's position. We continued the respectful conversation looking for ways in which we might cooperate with each other amid the violence outside our meeting place.

Both the Buddha and the Christ were deeply concerned about peace, but each framed the peace issues differently. The two ways do not cancel each other out, but they do result in different emphases and approaches to the resolution of violence. The Buddhist tradition comes out of India and China and represents a distinct definition and approach to peacemaking.

The Hindu tradition out of which Buddhism first emerged begins with the concept of peace as *shanti*, or inner peace and tranquility. In his Firth Lectures John Macquarrie put it well: "*Santi* [sic] means spiritual contentment, a profound integration of the inward life of man."[14] As an ideal it is realized in the village setting, where at the end of the day members of the village gather to chant the prayer, "*Shanti, shanti* . . ." blessing the activities of the day and praying for its continuing harmony. The Chinese *wa* and the Japanese *heiwa* connote this same sense of harmony, and serenity, not only as a political ideal but as a holistic tranquility in society and nature.

Although there are many cultural traditions in Buddhism, the teachings of Thich Nhat Hahn, a Vietnamese monk who has made a significant impact on the American peace movement, is a good representative example of this East Asian tradition.

Nhat Hahn is a compassionate, self-giving, advocate of just peace who insists that the proof of any ideology, including his own, is in the doing! In his *Living Buddha, Living Christ* he writes, "For the Buddha to be present in the Sangha [community], we must practice in a way that keeps his teachings alive . . . [And] for Christians, the way to make the Holy Spirit truly present in the church is to practice thoroughly what Jesus lived and taught."[15] His quiet admonition reminds us that according to our Christian Scripture also the presence of the Holy Spirit is manifested in activity and movement.

Hahn views the human problem as one of inner peace and anger management. Anger, he says, is a negative energy that must be transformed into a more positive energy like empathy, love, and compassion through self-control. Anger is not caused by an "enemy" outside of us but rather by our ignorance ("wrong perception"). It is "also rooted in desire, pride, agitation, and suspicion. The roots of anger are in ourselves."[16] To overcome anger we must cultivate the "energy of mindfulness," and when we do this "the first insight we have is that the main cause of our suffering, of our misery [anger], is not the other person—it is the seed of anger in us."[17] Peace for Hahn is primarily "inner peace," which when achieved enables us to live in harmony with others.

This is a profound psychological insight, and there are obvious parallels to it in the teachings of Jesus. But this framing of the issues, much too briefly described here, leads Nhat Hahn to a different approach to peacemaking than Jesus. Hahn's non-dualistic perspective leads him to focus on the self-care and improvement of the individual, which he calls "mindfulness," as our primary responsibility for building world peace. The way to peace, in the words of the Dalai Lama's forward to his *Peace is Every Step*, is through the "internal transformation of individuals" by the techniques of meditation and training in mindfulness. Hahn explains,

> I am not saying that someone who viciously attacks us should not be disciplined. But what is most important is that we first take care of the seeds of negativity in ourselves. Then if someone needs to be helped or disciplined, we will do so out of compassion, not anger and retribution.[18]

Hahn's explanation provides a bridge between the teachings of Jesus and the Buddha at the level of social ethics. Jesus' deeply religious presuppositions lead him to a different emphasis. He saw the problem as more than a private spiritual uneasiness, negative energy, or "misery" whose flame must be cooled.

For Jesus, peace exists as a state of being between oneself and the *other*, which includes both God and fellow humans in a community of shalom. In Jesus' world "the other" has a real existence, an ontological quality that factors it into making peace. Quintessential in his self-awareness, or "mindfulness," is awareness of an empowering Other who not only sets the boundaries for personal relations but provides the energy/dynamic for self-control.

While Jesus recognized the need for inner peace and tranquility and often withdrew from the crowds to meditate and pray, he viewed the problem to be resolved by peace-*making* as an offensive act of hostility and the resentment-alienation which results from it. For Jesus peace requires negotiation with the opponent, not merely meditation and the transformation of one's own negativity. Without reconciliation to the opponent, one's own inner peace is marred.

Further, speaking in the Hebrew tradition, Jesus made *justice*, not serenity, the essential element and condition of *shalom*. As has been demonstrated in the history of Asian cultures, the weakness of harmony (*wa*) as the essence of peace is that it tends to rationalize and maintain a static, hierarchical concept of social justice, which favors the powerful. Justice as Jesus understood it is attained when the well-being of even the most vulnerable in the community is promoted, and true harmony is possible only as justice is realized.

On this point the contrast between the style of Jesus and the Buddha is striking. The Buddha's solution to his own lack of *shanti* (peace) was to ignore the socio-political realities of society and to rid himself of all desire to be part of its value system. Jesus, by contrast, identified himself with the vulnerable masses in their poverty and taught that true peace comes through sharing the wealth of the earth.

JESUS AND PACIFISM

In the West, Buddha has been associated with meditative traditions like Hinduism, and Jesus has been associated with a more active pacifist tradition. There has been ongoing debate about his identity as a pacifist, and indeed this essay at least touches on the debate. The question is largely anachronistic since many of the issues that define pacifism in today's setting were at best incipient in Jesus' day. Thus for example the questions of pacifism and "just war" as we know them were not yet in view. The Jewish nation was a theocracy ruled by a priestly hierarchy. War could be justified only as "holy war," as in the case of the Maccabean wars of a century earlier. When Yahweh, the Warrior, called to war, there was no room for a pacifist response or to question its justice.

The just war theory was expounded in the fifth century by Augustine and continued in both the Roman Catholic and Eastern Orthodox traditions during the centuries following. The theory attempts to adapt the nonviolent teaching of the church to its new status as the religion of the Roman Empire, and could hardly have been in Jesus' mind. It assumes that wars can be lawful and essentially limited to self-defense, but with the development of modern global technology both of these assumptions have been thrown into grave doubt.

The words *pacifism* and *pacifist* have become common in our vocabulary only within the last century. In dictionary language a pacifist is one who "strongly and actively opposes conflict and especially war." Nineteenth-century objections to violence and war were usually referred to as nonresistance and defenselessness. But early in the twentieth century a more socially active opposition to war and violence developed, which was dubbed "pacifism."[19]

Pacifism connoted an active sociopolitical objection to war, whereas nonresistance indicated a more passive submission to violence without retaliation. In the intervening century these two positions became confused, and pacifism was often criticized as a passive response to social evil. Not even the civil rights movement and the anti-Vietnam War protests of the 1960s have completely changed this impression in the popular mind.

The civil rights movement, however, did add other words and agendas to the peacebuilding repertory. Martin Luther King Jr., a Christian pacifist, appealed to and used the nonviolent techniques of Mahatma Gandhi to protest and change the segregation laws of the United States. Specifically he adopted Gandhi's practice of *non-cooperation*, or *nonviolent resistance* to the social mores and legal regulations that defined systemic violence. This pacifistic intervention highlighted the importance of justice for peacebuilding, but it also initiated nonviolent conflict and added new dimensions of *conflict resolution* to the peacemaker's task.

So was Jesus a pacifist? He clearly taught that we should not retaliate for injury done to us, but he hardly fits the image of a contemporary pacifist protesting or organizing against social and political violence. Or is he more accurately characterized as nonresistant?

Certainly his whole life and ministry were characterized by a non-retaliatory spirit, and he did not challenge the military government of Rome. But the childhood picture of a "gentle Jesus meek and mild" does not fit him. He could and did become angry at the hypocrisy and abuse he witnessed in Jewish society. And he did engage in acts of civil/religious disobedience challenging the temple system. One could almost visualize his "triumphal entry" into the Jerusalem temple at the end of his life as a protest march. But as I have repeatedly said, the question itself involves us in making historical analogies and leaves us with ethical and cultural questions of authentic contextualization.

A Jesus Style

Since in this brief treatment of the subject we are going to concentrate on the ethical and social aspects of Jesus' words, perhaps we should note immediately that for Jesus the separation of the spiritual and the social was unthinkable. That is vital to understanding his style. In this sense he too was, in Buddhist terms, a "non-dualist." While he does not seem to have preached many "evangelistic" sermons during his ministry or "saved many souls," the very setting of his ministry presupposes that God is at work in the process, and that reconciling people to God necessarily involves their living at peace as the people of God. The two aspects of spiritual and social are simply dimensions of one relationship and cannot be separated, as Jesus indicated when he included love of neighbor with the "first commandment" to love God (Mark 12:28-34; Luke 10:27). Indeed, it is not even clear which comes first, for as 1 John says, love of neighbor is the covenant requirement without which one cannot truthfully claim to love God (4:20-21).

Actually little in what Jesus taught is brand-new. In fact, he claims to represent the fulfillment of the long tradition of the Law and the prophets of ancient Israel. Parallels to some of his aphorisms can be found also in the scriptures of other religions. Jesus' unique peacemaking perspective stems from his character, stance, and contextual situation—his *gestalt* or *style*, and not the novelty or brilliance of his sayings.

In a word, it is Jesus' unwavering trust in the goodness of God, his consistently nonviolent respect for others, his unfailing compassion for his fellow humans, and his resolute fearlessness in the face of death that gives his example dynamic relevance far beyond his first-century life. All these are summed up in Dietrich Bonhoeffer's characterization of him as "the Man for others."[20]

His *consistent nonviolence* is most evident in his refusal to see any other person as "enemy." He insisted on a single attitude toward friend and foe, seeing both as "neighbor." And he commanded his disciples to follow God's example by consistently showing good will toward both friend and enemy. The essence of his life example is distilled in his dying prayer that God would forgive his executors.

In his now famous sermon, "Beyond Vietnam," given at the Riverside Church in 1967, Martin Luther King recommended that this Jesus' kind of nonviolence be adopted toward the Vietnamese enemy.

> Here is the true meaning and value of compassion and nonviolence, where it helps us to see the enemy's point of view, to hear his questions, to know his assessment of ourselves. For from his view we may in-

deed see the basic weakness of our own condition, and if we are mature, we may learn and grow and profit from the wisdom of the brothers who are called the opposition.

To such nonviolent respect we must add Jesus' *compassion*, which is expressed in his identification with the most vulnerable in society—"the poor." He was born among them, and he called them the beloved of God long before Mahatma Gandhi called them *harijan*. He was never condescending toward them but at the same time never indulged them. Indeed, respect and compassion may well be a better translation of *agape* than love.

And to compassion we must also add a third characteristic of Jesus, namely, *his consistent and fearless honesty and confrontation with the religious and political powers of his day*. He is perhaps the best example of Gandhi's well-known observation that non-cooperation, or nonviolent resistance to evil, is as important as doing the good thing. Jesus' unwillingness to compromise or condone wrongdoing was precisely the political reason for his execution on the cross. He would not overlook the Sanhedrin's duplicity, and he would not kowtow to Pilate, who ordered him executed.

These features that characterize his identity are what Christians refer to as the form or gestalt of Sonship, and they are possible only through the intimacy of his relationship to "the Father." His self-identity and self-confidence rested in his self-submission to the Father's will. This according to all the accounts was the secret of his incredible humility and courage. And it was in his peerless self-giving on the cross that his disciples came to see the very face of God.

But if the cross were the full symbol of Jesus' style, he would be just one more martyr example—perchance the greatest, but only a martyr nonetheless. The full pattern of his life and ministry must include his disciples' witness to his resurrection. His immediate disciples and those who have followed him throughout the centuries continue to experience the power of his "name" (Acts 3:6). Or in the words of Paul, Jesus, the "living being" has become "a life-giving spirit" (1 Cor. 15:45) changing lives and reconciling enemies.

In a mysterious way that his disciples could only describe as his being raised from among the dead, he continues to be present at the peacemaker's table. Or in the words of the letter to the Hebrews, he continues the pioneering task of opening the way of faith to live beyond the fear of death.

Reconciliation and Shalom

Finally, what kind of peacemaking is implied in Jesus' words, "Blessed are the peacemakers?" Is peacemaking predominantly a social and political activity, in which people are enabled to live in peace and tolerance? Or is it fundamentally a spiritual task of reconciling sinners to God, as the revivalist tradition holds? Is peacemaking the quieting of hostilities (conflict resolution)? Is it maintenance of "law and order" in society? Can there be true peace without justice in society? And if not, does peacemaking include the work of achieving systemic justice? Are nonviolent protestors against injustice to be classed as peacemakers even though they sometimes stir up violent responses? However one answers these questions, the style of Jesus' peacemaking has relevance.

We noted earlier in the chapter that there are clear differences in the styles and approach to peace and peacemaking between the teachings of Buddhism and Christianity. Indeed, within Christianity itself there are a variety of vantage points from which to understand the meaning of Christ's words. However, his style is distinctly related to his concept of peace itself. At the core of peacemaking is the idea of *reconciliation*—the restoration of a community of respect, trust, and interdependence. The occasion for this becomes clear in its cultural context.

The cultural setting of Jesus' concept of peace is the extended family or tribe where kinship and interdependence provide a base for social structure and relationships. The Hebrew nation identified itself as "the children of Israel" and viewed some of the surrounding tribes as related through ancient kinship ties as "children of Abraham." Peace in such a society was essentially a communal or relational concept.

The greeting of stranger or friend with "Shalom" was a pledge of honorable relationship. Of course it includes the idea of inner as well as social tranquility, but shalom (peace) exists in society when the proper relationships of respect and honor result in fairness, compassion, and integrity, which promote trust and security.

So Jesus' concept and style of peace is inherently social. It has to do with neighborly relations—the proper moral functioning of community. By its intrinsic nature the peace of which Jesus speaks denotes more than an inner serenity, freedom from anxiety or guilt, or an intimate spiritual relationship to God. It is an order of just or righteous interpersonal relationships reflecting the character and will of the God.

Jesus universalized this familial concept of peace when, for example, he declared the Jerusalem temple "a house of prayer for *all people.*" He stated that the blessings of his Father's kingdom are not limited to the children of Abraham and included enemies (Gentiles, foreigners) in the love commandment. He pictured God as the Father of the whole human family sending rain and sunshine on "the evil and the good," and when he challenged his followers to be "perfect as God is perfect" (Matt. 5:48), he called them to a standard of impartial good will and justice as peacemakers spreading God's shalom. Of course, harmony (*wa*), serenity, and security are implicit results of shalom, but for Jesus the concept of justice is embedded in the concept of shalom, and genuine inner peace stems from it.

Peacemaking, therefore, is the restoration of shalom. At the heart of Jesus' concept is the idea of reconciliation, the restoration of relationship. *Repentance* and *forgiveness* are closely associated with it. At its heart it is a movement from violence and hostility leading to rapprochement of offender and victim. Where shalom has been disrupted through personal or systemic offense and injustice, the breach can only be restored through a mutual rapprochement of repentance and forgiveness. This is the work of peacemaking.

Insofar as possible this reconciliation includes the healing of alienation and the restoration of respect and trust. It is more than re-balancing power relationships, satisfying the victim's need for "closure," or the therapeutic rehabilitation of the offender. And as has often been pointed out in connection with the work of the South African Truth and Reconciliation Commission, genuine reconciliation requires the restoration of truth in human relations. Thus the well-known words attributed to Jesus in John 14:6, "No one comes to the Father except through me" point to him as the *reconciler* of humanity to each other and to God.

Chapter 4

FRAMING JESUS' MESSAGE

The concept of "framing" messages was introduced to the American populous during the national political elections in 2004. The linguist George Lakoff pointed out that although the opposing political parties were using the same political phrases and talking about the same economic processes, they were actually implying quite different political and economic programs.

Lakoff observed, for example, that those who advocated the Iraq war framed its "metaphors to kill" as *self-defense* against nuclear threat, or a *rescue* of the Iraqi people from torture and misrule by a savage dictator. In neither case was it acknowledged that in pursuit of the war's goals millions of innocent Iraqi people were being killed by the American bombs. Those who disapproved the war found it difficult to come up with effective counter-frames that highlighted this reality. And Lakoff pointed out that it is these "frames" that determine how people hear what is being said.

In like manner the religious and political leaders of Jesus' day framed their message in the traditional social-political presuppositions and metaphors that justified self-interest as the root motivation for action. They presumed that the diverse and scattered Jewish people were Yahweh's special nation (kingdom) through whom God would bring justice and peace to the earth, and read the Torah in that frame.

Jesus referred to their framing as what had "been said to those in ancient times" (Matt. 5:21ff), i.e., how Moses had been understood and taught, and then pointed to a different perspective for understanding the commandment referred to.

How did people hear Jesus? One of his common admonitions to his audiences was, "Let those who have ears to hear listen." What was he really saying? He used the lingua franca of his age—its historical and mythical allusions, its political idioms, its cultural assumptions and metaphors. His teachings were framed in the metaphors of an ancient religious worldview. Yet when compared to the common political wisdom, his frame of reference was different. His metaphors for God and God's intention for how the world should work imply a different framing from the religious leaders of his day.

Added to the difficulty of projecting ourselves back into Jesus' time and culture is the dissonance of contemporary Christian interpretations of his life and significance. We must sort through not only the interpretative frames of ancient culture but also the different contemporary global perspectives, and the frames of competing religious factions in our own society—the liberal frames, evangelical frames, Catholic frames, Anabaptist frames, and the like.

In the following chapters we will attempt to explore how Jesus' different framing of the issues results in a moral worldview that defines his unique style of peacemaking. What we will need to remember is that all our images are cultural translations framed to make him relevant to our time and needs. Except in the broad outlines, what he actually said and how he intended his words to be applied, even in his own first-century setting, are open to debate as history demonstrates.

Notions about his personality and what he taught vary just as widely as do artistic portrayals. For most he is a God figure, a religious icon, a close friend, a loving savior from guilt, an example of suffering endurance, and many others. These contemporary impressions serve for personal reflection, reverence, example, and encouragement. By and large he has been pictured as an object of religious piety and an example of traditional personal virtues—family values, honesty, thrift, kindness, generosity, and the like. The minority image that pictures him as a prophetic leader and teacher of radical nonviolence has never won recognition as a realistic alternative for social action even among the majority of Christians.

It is understandable that we should picture him in images familiar to our culture. But truth be told, we know little about him as a personality. The historical person and his significance remain indistinct. The Gospels are not biographies in our modern sense of the word describing his personality. Most of our historical data are in the form of vignettes and teachings. One does get a general impression or gestalt of this man from Galilee, but we have no definitive biographical picture of him. As for his teachings, most of them are in parables, aphorisms, and commands as we have noted earlier, and even his disciples were often puzzled.

Jesus did not write textbooks, commentaries, or practical manuals of wisdom. He did not offer ethical or theological rationalizations to implement his wisdom sayings. We are left not only to try to understand what he was saying in his own historical setting but also to ask what his teaching and example might look like in our very different modern setting.

His teachings assume a traditional first-century cultural situation of political dictatorship and military occupation. He and his compatriots were "subjects" not "citizens" of Rome, and we are left to apply his counsel to twenty-first-century democracy. What metaphors for God might Jesus use if he were teaching today? What political responsibilities might he enjoin in our more egalitarian society? And what examples of nonviolent response and peacemaking might he use?

We can only bridge the gap between first-century Jewish society and our technological cultures with comparable analogies. Nevertheless we need to check the authenticity of our analogies by a constant search to understand the historical reality on which they are based. Thus in this chapter we will attempt to frame Jesus in his own first-century Jewish setting before we ask what his teaching and example might mean for peacebuilding today.

KINGSHIP—THE FRAME FOR JESUS' MESSAGE

Jesus framed his message of peace in the social and political patterns of his time. Judea considered itself a theocratic nation-state even though it was under occupation by the pagan Roman government. God was king ruling from the temple, and Israel was God's nation or kingdom representing God's authority among the nations. Israel's laws, both religious and political, were considered God's will for his universal kingdom, and Israel was God's agent to make known this will among the nations. Jesus came announcing, as had John the Baptizer before him, that God's just rule exists among humankind for the taking (Luke 17:20-21). The good news was that in Jesus' appearance "the kingdom of heaven/God has come near" (Matt. 10:7) and is being offered to all who will follow him. (Matt. uses heaven, the realm of God, as a metonym for God. Compare Luke 4:43.)

Jesus did not coin a new term when he proclaimed the arrival of the God's reign. The kingdom, or rule, of God in its broadest sense was understood as human society under the beneficent covenant of the Creator that sets the boundaries for human life in the universe. As we pray in the Lord's Prayer, it is God's will "done on earth as it is in heaven." This was the meaning of "kingdom of God" that Jesus inherited and announced as imminent in his ministry.

This covenant rule had not been accomplished under the tutelage of Hebrew monarchs, but the Jewish leaders still clung to the promise that under Israel's imperial primacy it could be achieved. Jesus proclaimed the good news, or "gospel" that its universalization was about to be inaugurated—but not by imperial power. The kingdom, or reign, of God as intended under the covenant with Israel, was about to be inaugurated through his nonviolent messianic ministry.

There were many versions of the kingdom alive in first-century Palestine when Jesus began to teach, and Jesus' version was not immediately clear even to his followers. The Jewish religious leaders assumed that the ancient empire of their great king David provided the pattern for establishing the reign of God. Most, if not all, previous messiahs understood the metaphor of political kingship as a literal reign of God over the earth under the agency of national Israel. Jerusalem would be the world capitol and the temple would be the sacred center from which God ruled. God would bring in universal peace through heavenly military intervention and thus establish shalom despite the counter-violence of humans.

For example, according to a passage from the War Scroll of the Qumran Community, Israel should prepare to "rule over the kingdom of the nations! Sovereignty shall be to the Lord and everlasting dominion to Israel" (1 QM 12:15). Other less militant versions from the prophets pictured a time of God's universal beneficent sovereignty, but all based universal peace on the violent intervention of God as the all-powerful Sovereign.

So Jesus used this well-known metaphor of kingship, but he gave it a nonviolent frame that implies a quite different view of God's sovereignty. Even the message of John the Baptizer, who introduced Jesus to the crowds at Jordan, assumed that God would exercise violent power and judgment to establish the kingdom (Matt. 3:10ff). But quite in contrast to this expectation, Jesus presented the rule of God as *an offer that could be rejected*. Its coming presented a crisis, but it was a crisis of decision not of violent imposition. When Jesus sent his disciples out to announce to the villagers of Galilee that "The kingdom of God has come near to you," they were simply to warn the people of the consequences and leave if the offer was rejected (Luke 10: 10-11). Shalom comes as an offer, not as a coercive command.

WHAT KIND OF A KINGDOM?

The accounts of Jesus' ministry are set in the context of the question whether Jesus or John is the Messiah who will usher in the kingdom of God. Luke tells us that John's appearance preaching in the wilderness raised peoples' expectations, and they were wondering whether John might be the Messiah (Luke 3:15). This puzzlement raises the question about the essential nature of God's rule and shalom. Will it be manifest as a rule of coercion and judgment as John announced? Or will it be mediated as reconciliation and healing? Matthew relates how John himself, as he sat in prison awaiting execution, had second thoughts about Jesus because he was not implementing the violent judgment of God on King Herod and the unfaithful religious leaders of Judaism (Matt. 11:2-6).

The kingdom of God cannot be described in rational institutional terms, but Jesus' answer to John's inquiry gives us a clue to its nature. It can only be defined in terms of literal self-giving acts of social responsibility and compassion. And Jesus did describe it in parables. He told his disciples that the parables were to reveal the secret nature of the kingdom, and thus we need to highlight what kind of images he used in them. Following this lead, Ramsey Michaels notes that alongside the traditional political and military images, Jesus put "gentler images of planting and growth, fishing, women baking bread, landowners finding treasures, or merchants buying pearls."[21] And we might add that these are the images of extended family and the dynamics of a shame-oriented society. Herein lay the "secret," what Michaels refers to as the "twist," that Jesus gave to the metaphor.

Jesus' description of the kingdom of God does not accentuate the legal aspects of the political metaphor. This suggests that peacemaking is not a legal balancing of power advantages but a realignment of severed relations. Further, the sanctions of the kingdom of God are not *extrinsically* imposed punishments made by an arbitrary all-powerful monarch. Neither are they democratically enacted political penalties to satisfy the latest citizens' poll. They are, rather, the restraints of the created moral and natural order. They simply mark what threatens life in a community of justice and peace—what is not life enhancing in the community.

Human political systems are based on imposed legal sanctions and enforced by violence. By contrast God's ultimate control is based on the *implicit consequence* of both natural and moral evil rather than punitive vindication of legislated conduct. The purpose of God's rule is the well-being of creation, and if God's law is transgressed, its vindication is achieved in transformation and reconciliation, not in vindictive punishment (retaliation) of the violator. And ultimately according to Jesus' model divine sovereignty will be accomplished by the power of resurrection. It is displayed in *victory over death*, which all the New Testament writers regard as the consequence of disobedience to God's authority, not by the violent enforcement of the death penalty.

Jesus' reply to Pilate when he was on trial for his life epitomizes his view. In contrast to the imperial power of Rome he declared, "My kingdom is not from this world. If my kingdom were from this world, my followers would be fighting to keep me from being handed over to the Jews" (John 18:36). Often these words have been misinterpreted to mean that Jesus' kingdom is an individual spiritual reality. But his many references to the kingdom of God throughout his ministry make clear that he was referring to the moral and spiritual character of his authority. It was not built on power and violence like earthly kingdoms.

This distinction between God's reign as a proffered blessing of peace and the kingdoms of this world that are established by violent force illuminates a crucial aspect of Jesus' concept of peacemaking. It gives us a clue for distinguishing between "nonviolent coercion" and violence in his teachings. (See chapter 7.) Speaking in an ethnic, shame-oriented society where the honor code, such as we still see operative in groups like Hamas and Hezbollah, demands revenge and retaliation, Jesus redefines honor in terms of the Beatitudes. The meek, impoverished, naively honest, long-suffering, and forgiving are to be classed as the honorable (blessed) in the kingdom, and their vindication comes not by vengeance but by righting the wrongs that oppress them.

To be sure, Jesus speaks of God's "wrath" and of the dire consequences of evil behaviors. Throughout the Bible the consequences of evil are spoken of as God's judgment, and their inevitability is spoken of as "the day of God's wrath" and even vengeance. Using the metaphor of Gehenna, the smoldering garbage dump outside the walls of Jerusalem (Matt. 5:22), Jesus says that those who live a violent, self-serving offensive life will suffer the consequences of worthlessness, which is waste and ruin on the garbage dump of history. Such self-destruction is the intrinsic consequence of misguided and destructive lives.

For Jesus, then, sanctions of the kingdom of God are the consequences intrinsic in harmful behavior, not extrinsic political penalties assigned like a fine for wrong political action. These consequences of evil are waste, ruin, destruction characterized in Romans 6:23 as "the wages of sin [which is] death"—and not retaliatory legal punishment. The sovereignty of God's rule, which establishes shalom, is demonstrated in the inevitability of these consequences and not in the vindication of righteousness by punitive vengeance.

Recognizing the Culture Gap

The gap between the traditional theocratic society in which Jesus' teaching was situated and today's secular democracies (though increasingly they exist amid reviving theocracies) is often overlooked by contemporary readers. How might this concept of theocratic authority implicit in the phrase *kingdom of God* translate in a democracy? And what are the implications for peacemaking?

Assuming the theocratic model of his time and culture, Jesus used the monarchal metaphor to describe God's rule, but he modified the nature of that authority and its prosecution. God's authority is not imposed by political fiat backed with violent power. Rather, it is intrinsic and nonviolent. As "King of the Universe," an honorific Jewish title, God enforces his authority by the dynamic of the creative order, and it is experienced as the consequences that follow behavior. It is a "spiritual" reality and direction to be responded to in freedom.

In the medieval period, Western Christendom continued to use the theocratic political model, representing itself as God's kingdom ruled by symbiotic religious and political authorities. It did not, however, recognize the significance of Jesus radical modification when it wedded the spiritual and temporal authorities. God's sovereign authority was understood in traditional terms as the threat of violent power literally administered by religious and political agents. Jesus became judge and king ruling not only by spiritual but also by temporal power. The Ten Commandments became the grist of political legislation, and the Beatitudes became the spiritual ideal for the monasteries.

When Western Christian political thought moved to a democratic model, the idea of political, or even religious, authority through a divinely appointed ruler was reversed. Authority was transferred to and vested in the people and not in God-appointed rulers (an appointment that gave them absolute authority). At the same time, the authority of church and state was compartmentalized, and the authority of elected secular governments was limited to implementing the rational and unalienable rights of "life, liberty and the pursuit of happiness." But this authority was still attributed to God, and both church and state still assumed that secular government, which protects the church, has the same violent prerogatives under God.

Inherent in this concept is a new kind of human relationship between individuals. No longer is there a privileged class of rulers (political or religious). When and if God speaks, he speaks through the democratic processes and for the welfare of the people, not in direct communication through and for the advantage of the rulers.

In the early years of the twentieth century some theologians suggested that we should now speak of the "democracy of God," but it was not at all clear how God's authority would be exercised in such a model. Surely God is more than an elected president! While it is seldom stated explicitly, this inversion implies that *God wills the ultimate good of the people*. At its best this is the ideological basis for a democratic order in which God's authority is exercised as "Abba," neither as president nor a dictatorial potentate.

These political implications of the democratic paradigm led to a shift in the way the moral rightness of behavior was defined and likewise in the theological rationale for moral sanctions. Virtuous, or morally good, behavior was no longer defined by the edict of a divine despot.[22] Rather, God, the loving Parent-Creator, decreed it *because* it is good for the creatures "in God's image." Assuming that God is for the people, and that their well-being is the preeminent divine concern—that is, that "God is love"—moral behavior comes to be defined as that which enhances human well-being. Anthropological considerations become the focus in the sphere of public morality, and God's relation to the political process takes on a less direct kingly character. It is arguable that the Hebrew-Christian tradition implicitly introduced these subtle but crucial changes, but they should not be equated with the political paradigm presupposed in the early church's concept of "the kingdom of God."

So how shall we translate the meaning of that kingdom in our modern anthropocentric world? How shall we understand the power and authority of God in the peacemaking process, which is essentially a political process? The medieval church operating with a theocratic paradigm attempted to limit the destructive violence of war by issuing edicts. The *Pax Dei* (Peace of God) and later the *Treuga Dei* (Truce of God) specified the noncombatants who should not be harmed and the holy days (Sundays and Lent) when the fighting tribes should declare a temporary truce. Such religious dictates were of limited value even then and of no pragmatic value today!

Shall we, then, as peacemakers in the name of Jesus promote the welfare of humankind—protest war, the death penalty, and abortion? Shall we join political negotiations for less violence? Try to interrupt the trauma circle that leads to violent retaliation? Protest injustice nonviolently? Shall we, like the late Clarence Jordan, create a new Koinonia Farm where kingdom justice is the rule as a critique of the existing political order? Shall we foster shalom by supporting Habitat for Humanity and Fair Trade organizations that commit themselves to righting the economic imbalance and injustice which oppress the working poor? Or in our highly specialized society might it imply that peacemaking indicates a frame of mind and heart that seeks the welfare of others in whatever we do?

We will pursue the implications of the culture gap between Jesus' kingdom language and our contemporary Western world in chapter 8, but before we do that we need to examine further Jesus' view of God as the ultimate sovereign power, which he had inherited from Jewish culture. How can Jesus' message be related to power?

Chapter 5

JESUS AND ISRAEL'S VIEW OF GOD

While Christians of all denominations claim the New Testament and teachings of Jesus as their ultimate authority, they still frame their interpretation of God's power and authority in Old Testament metaphors. They continue to base their view of God and peacemaking on the theological premises of Israel, which predate Jesus.

In this view God is "king" above all earthly authorities. His just vengeance, although mysterious in its workings, is legitimated by his superior knowledge, which is not to be questioned, and his power to accomplish whatever he wills. His special regard for the people of Israel is extended to include all those who accept Jesus as the Messiah, although for some national Israel still maintains a favorite position. According to this paradigm, peace and peacemaking still are grounded on the ultimate threat of powerful intervention.

It is precisely this power metaphor and the political paradigm based on it that Jesus challenged. *He challenged the view of God as the sovereign power who intervenes with violence to overrule human irresponsibility and enforce shalom.* He redefined the divine-human equation. God remains sovereign, but he does not sanctify violence by intervening with violent miracles. For example, he did not save Jesus from the cross.

Neither did he keep his temple from being destroyed by the Romans, nor save the Jews from final defeat at Masada. Jesus views God's power not as violent intervention but as the nonviolent immanent dynamic of *agape*.

GOD AS "ALMIGHTY"

In the Hebrew tradition God was seen as an almighty, just, and compassionate king. "King of the universe" is still a common Jewish form of address for God. Israel's God, Yahweh, who created the universe and determined its natural and social order, was their king. The Law (Torah) that regulated both the ritual and moral life of Israel was God's "statutes," and Israel's national life style was to represent God's character among the nations by keeping Yahweh's statutes. Thus these commandments defined God's character as well as his relationship to the "holy nation."

A tacit implication in this metaphor of ancient kingship was also God's favoritism—a precedent for Christian exclusivism. His mercy although universal was biased toward his covenant people. His compassion was experienced as mercy in much the same sense as Allah is the "All Merciful" in the Islamic tradition. Given his transcendent status and power, God could afford to be merciful to the extent that it did not threaten his sovereignty. While his punitive justice might be experienced for several generations, the prophet promises that his faithful mercy extends to all generations.

In this metaphor of sovereign kingship the nation's shalom was found in obeying the sovereign's covenant commands. Disorder and conflict were caused by breaking the King's commands—by sinning against God who established the social codes. Malicious harm against the neighbor was sin against Yahweh, and the offense required reconciliation with God as well as neighbor. Also implicit in the metaphor was the assumption that the nation's enemies were God's enemies! Thus if the Jewish nation would repent its sins and faithfully obey the covenant law, God could be expected to intervene, violently if necessary, to overcome their enemies and establish his rightful hegemony through their agency.

Israel's understanding of the nature and character of God's holiness shifted considerably through the centuries. When it emerged as a national group its leader, Joshua, visualized Yahweh as a mighty warrior leading his people in a holy war of invasion to destroy the idolatrous cultures of Canaan, contemporary Palestine. This picture of God as King and Holy Warrior continued as a sub-theme throughout Israel's history. *God was imaged as a just and beneficent dictator who used violent power when necessary to overcome evil and re-establish compassionate justice.* Accordingly, Israel assumed its right to use violence under God's direction to establish God's reign over the nations. Although under the domination of Rome at the time, this was the religious assumption of Judaism in the first century.

At its best, then, God's "Almightiness" meant that God transcends all limitation and is totally in control of the universe. Power is understood as both creative and coercive force, and God's control is manifested both in sustaining creation and overcoming the destructive powers of evil through violent intervention when necessary. Love, which controls God's power, is defined as compassion, which modifies retributive justice. God's violence is justified by the ultimate transcendent peace that it is expected to accomplish. However, no matter how merciful and compassionate God is portrayed to be, violence is justified in the pursuit of peace.

Jesus' View of God as "Abba"

Every culture enshrines its highest moral ideals in its deity, or deities, and these become the guide and justification for moral action. For example, Gandhi explicitly appealed to the example of Krishna in the *Bhagavad Gita* as source and example of ahimsa. And although he also reverenced Jesus and the Sermon on the Mount, it is debatable in the end whether his paradigm of nonviolence was not more influenced by Krishna than Christ. In this same manner Jesus too claimed simply to be doing what he saw the Father doing.

As a Jew, his whole self-identity was tied up with his understanding of and relation to the God of Israel, who commanded his people to "be holy as I am holy" (Lev. 20: 26). Holiness refers to the whole character of God that sets the divine ideal apart from the human cultural reality. God's holiness is seen in the impartiality of God's good will, justice, love, and compassion for all humankind. Thus Jesus' intimate prayer recorded in Matthew, in which he thanks the Father that he has been chosen to reveal the divine character, points to Jesus' crucial significance for understanding God. And Jesus adds, "no one knows the Father except the Son and anyone to whom the Son chooses to reveal him (Matt. 11:25-27). This gives special impact to his words in the seventh beatitude: "Blessed are the peacemakers, for they will be called the *children of God*" (Matt. 5:9).

It is significant, then, to note that his basic characterization of God is love (*agape*) and forgiveness. This does not mean that he denied the power of God or overlooked the impartiality of God's justice. The opposite of love is not sovereign power but rather a deficit of compassion and a resort to retaliatory power to enforce the divine will. What we need to observe is how he modifies the concept of power and the definition of justice. *The power of God is nonviolent and the justice of God is consequential and ultimate.* Jesus called God "Abba," which is an Aramaic term of parental intimacy. But Jesus' emphasis on God's fatherly concern does not imply that God is indulgent or weak. To say "Papa" does not diminish God's power or sovereignty.

The concept of God's protective parenthood is found in the prophets of Israel also. But Jesus' emphasizes the *impartiality* of God's *universal* paternity. To confess that the God of Israel is Ruler of the universe underscores God's universal power and sovereignty *and* implies universal concern and compassion. God is concerned for the salvation or good of all people—Jewish and Gentile—alike. The intimate family concern extends beyond Israel to include all humans. Israel's God is "Father" of the universe, and as we have seen, Jesus insisted that God's temple be the "house of prayer for all nations." Jesus recognized the legitimacy of the Jerusalem temple as symbol of Israel's special relation to God but did not identify God's paternity with Israel's national existence.

"*Abba*" implies the nonviolence of God's will for justice and the impartiality of his beneficence. Jesus taught that he had come to fulfill the law and the prophets, and that "not one letter or stroke of a letter" in the law would fail until his mission was accomplished (Matt. 5: 17-18), but he clearly did not equate the Father's justice with the literal commandments of the Jewish Torah. God is not a legalist and does not judge according to political standards of justice. And God is equally beneficent not only to Jew and Gentile but also to the just and the unjust. God is not biased toward the rich and famous; indeed God is the guardian of the poor and vulnerable. God's peace is characterized by fatherly, or family, justice.

Jesus' View of God's Power and Justice

According to our early sources Jesus did not give us a systematic theological description of God. His God is "the God of Israel" (Matt. 15:31)—the God of Abraham, Isaac, and Jacob, of Moses and the Prophets. For him God is "the Most High," the supreme, beneficent Power in the universe, who is the ultimate arbiter of vindictive justice. What is significant in Jesus' view is his modification of this traditional Hebrew image. Above all, as we have just seen, he refers to God as the "heavenly Father" (Matt. 6:32), and portrays him as the Forgiving One.

But Jesus also addressed God as "Lord of heaven and earth." This metaphor based on earthly kingship has resulted in attributing conventional notions of political power to God. Earthly lords use their power to rule by retaliatory force, whether implied or actual. If we read the metaphor as simply an echo of the Hebrew Scriptures, this is what might be implied. But is this the way in which God exercises lordship according to Jesus? Is God's authority based on the threat of violent intervention if disobeyed?

Jesus' cry of dereliction on the cross, "My God, my God why have you forsaken me," suggests that he wrestled to the very end with this question whether God would violently intervene to vindicate him. But his final words, "Into your hands I commend my life" indicate that faithful to his own spiritual insight, he did not expect such intervention.

So what was new in Jesus' view of God's power? He obviously conceived of God as the ultimate power and authority in the universe. But what kind of power? Is it the beneficent power of a dictator who controls by nonviolent coercion? Or is it the power of violent intervention to defeat evil forces bent on malicious destruction? Is it the power of natural law and moral authority to establish or restore justice in the social order? Or is it the persuasion of truth, which Gandhi and Martin Luther King held following Jesus' suggestion when he spoke of himself as the "true and living way?"

And how is peace related to power? Does it, as Mao suggests, come from the end of a gun? Does it come through the rational rule of law? Or does it result from living according to the truth—"walking in the light" as John puts it? This is obviously an important question for those who wish to understand Jesus' words about being peacemakers. The epistolary literature of the New Testament cannot be used to establish the exact teachings of the historical Jesus, but the letters do reflect how Jesus was understood by his earliest followers and thus give us our best clue to an overall framing of his sayings.

Both apostles John and Peter, who represent two different traditions in the early church, understood Jesus' view of God's power as preeminently the power of *agape* (love). Agape was not the common Greek word used for love, and its meaning must be gathered from its use in the New Testament literature. Cardinal Joseph Ratzinger, now Pope Benedict XVI, has aptly noted that in the writings of John truth and agape love are identical. His words are worth quoting here. "The concept of God attains its climax in the Johannine declaration: God is love (1 John 4:8). Truth and love are identical. *This sentence—if the whole of its demand is understood—is the surest guarantee of tolerance; of an association with truth, whose only weapon is itself and, thereby, love*" (italics mine).[23]

According to the Johannine tradition, Jesus understood God's power to be nonviolent. God is not a benevolent dictator who on occasion overrules human wickedness by coercive violence. Neither at the trial nor crucifixion of Jesus did God step in with violent power to vindicate his claims and guarantee the success of his cause. *Rather, God's action was demonstrated as agape in the healing, reconciling life and ministry of Jesus, and in the miraculous raising of Jesus from the dead when all seemed lost.*

Even God's judgment (the Greek word is *krisis*) comes not as violent vindication but as light that exposes those who are morally and spiritually blind (John 3:19; 9:39). Judgment is implicit in the consequences of human behavior, and God's judgment is understood as neither retaliatory nor vengeful. Justice is seen not in the perfect balance of retaliation for injury, but in the impartiality of judgment "according to [everyone's] deeds" (1 Pet. 1:17).

Like John, Peter sees the justice of God as demonstrated in God's "righteous forgiveness" (1 John 1:8-9) of all those who live in agapeic relationship. He appeals again and again to his readers to follow the nonviolent example of Jesus who suffered injustice on their behalf (2:21-24), and he writes that God's power was expressed by raising Jesus from the dead (1:3, 21; 3:21), not by violent interference that prevented his suffering and death. God planned for his self-identification with humanity through Jesus to be the means of transforming human suffering and death through resurrection.

In the opening lines of his first letter, Peter states that even before the "foundation of the world" God planned that evil and violence should be overcome not by greater violence but by the moral power of suffering and resurrection. The miracle of "resurrection," not human conniving, makes forgiveness a transformative possibility. Where there is genuine change of heart on the part of both the offender and the offended there is the miraculous possibility of future transformation. God's justice is demonstrated in love which forgives and empowers those who repent. This overview from John and Peter is a guide for authentically reading the character and implications of Jesus' life and teachings.

Forgiveness should not be equated with *absolution*, which according to the dictionary is a setting free from an obligation or consequence of guilt. Absolution, which the priest grants the sinner in the name of God, is commonly defined as the "remission of sins," which means cancelling the punishment that might be expected at the hands of God after death. In the world of human relationships, forgiveness does not release the offender from further obligation. While it creates the possibility for transformation in relationships, it does not simply cancel out intrinsic consequences of violent behavior.

Put in terms of social reconciliation and peace, God's power is seen in the reversal of the consequences of evil. This is the significance of Jesus' resurrection as the conclusion to his earthly life, not his crucifixion. The Gospel accounts do not close with the assurance that Jesus' immortal soul continues to exist in another spiritual realm despite his shameful execution. Rather, that God has vindicated Jesus' life and message here and now by reversing the consequences of violent judgment against him. This, of course, is portrayed as only the beginning of a historical struggle in which the world will be transformed and God's peace will eventually win.[24]

God's Forgiveness

God's forgiveness is not a new idea in Scripture introduced by Jesus, but in his teaching it takes on a more profound emphasis as a unique characteristic of divine love. In the Old Testament the question of forgiveness focuses on God's relationship to the nation Israel, not on people forgiving each other. It is portrayed as a pattern of leniency and restraint of violent power. This pattern is set in the exodus. Portrayed in anthropomorphic terms, God delivers and establishes Israel as a viable nation through miraculous feats of violent power. Israel in its petulant weakness fails to respond in grateful obedience and provokes God's "fierce anger." God who is a gracious Sovereign and recognizes their weakness restrains his anger but finally gives it vent in punitive vengeance only to relent when he sees their suffering. This pattern is repeated over and over.

This storyline is played out not as a political process but a natural process. God's anger is expressed as the natural and moral consequences of Israel's wrongdoing, breaking the covenant. Foolish political action, immoral and unjust social behavior, cultic pollution, and the like, lead to war and captivity, poverty, famine, and other natural disaster. Imaging wrongdoing as impurity, forgiveness is visualized as erasing or wiping away the filth. God cleans up the mess they have made of things, i.e., forgives them, if and when they are ready to change their ways.

Jesus does not use this beneficent dictator metaphor to frame his teachings about God's forgiveness. God's forgiveness is not pictured as a relenting mercy after bouts of anger but in the constant magnanimity of nature—the sun and rain falling on the just and the unjust. In this his disciples are to imitate their heavenly Father. They are to forgive not seven times but "seventy times seven"—a formula that means without counting. And he taught that God's love and good will are all-inclusive of friend and enemy alike. On the cross Jesus prayed God's forgiveness for his executors, and when it became clear that God was not going to intervene to justify or rescue him, he committed his life to God.[25]

This does not mean, in the words of the famous French philosopher, that "To know all is to forgive all," as though in the end no moral debits accrued. God's forgiveness does not tolerate or arbitrarily cancel the consequences of malicious, unjust, and selfish behavior. Selfish and violent behavior, which Mark refers to as lack of "salt" in human relationships (9: 49-50), can and does disrupt peace and destroy life. Jesus says that inherent consequences of evil attitudes and behavior can land one on the "garbage dump of the universe" (Mark 9:48; Matt. 5:22, 25). Jesus does not lower standards of justice. Rather he internalizes them as equal regard (love) for others as for oneself. A just peace (*shalom*) requires that people show the same regard and concern for enemies as for friends. His followers are to be *unlimited and impartial* ("perfect") in their love just as God is perfect (Matt. 5:43-48).

So if forgiveness is not to be understood simply as the amnesia or leniency of God, how are we to understand it? First, we should note that its purpose is more than the psychological or spiritual release from anger or resentment, although it does include that. *The goal of forgiveness as Jesus illustrated it in his parables is reconciliation and restoration of peace between alienated parties.* It may not restore the status quo ante. It cannot, for example, bring the murdered victim back to life or restore destroyed relationships, but where there is openness it can create the possibility for a new beginning.

This explains the strong emphasis on *metanoia* (repentance) in Jesus' teaching. *Repentance indicates a genuine will to change, and it is inherently necessary to receiving the forgiveness offered.* Repentance is not a formal or legal condition but an openness to respond positively to the forgiveness offered. When Jesus says that we cannot be forgiven if we do not forgive, he is not stating a legal requirement. Rather he recognizes that a lack of the grace to forgive others destroys our psychological and spiritual ability to recognize and accept forgiveness ourselves.

In his book, *Beyond Retribution*, Chris Marshall deftly summarizes the real meaning and purpose of forgiveness when he characterizes the South African Truth and Reconciliation Commission's work. He writes,

> It sought to restore dignity and personhood to victims and to offer a fresh start to offenders by making room for truth in place of silence, repentance in place of denial, mercy instead of retribution, and forgiveness instead of hatred.[26]

Forgiveness might be thought of as the alternative to retaliation in settling a moral score. One accepts the admission of guilt and sincere apology of the offender, which implies genuine change, in lieu of retaliation. Not vindication of one's honor or status by "getting even," but a mutually genuine willingness to forgive and be forgiven restores right relationship. In Jesus' teachings forgiveness is a step in the two-way adjustment of fractured relationships, and it is impossible to receive forgiveness if one is unwilling to give it.

By the same token, unwillingness on the part of either party to change stymies the full process of forgiveness and reconciliation. God's forgiveness can only be experienced as "longsuffering" or patience when repentance and reform are spurned. God's patience should not be mistaken for indulgence. God holds humans accountable for what they have been given. ("Of whom much is given, much is required" Luke 12:48.) The point seems to be rather that God does not demand a retaliatory balance for injury done before there can be forgiveness, but always stands ready to give us another chance when there is genuine repentance.

The new accent, then, falls on forgiveness and responding repentance as the prime requirements for achieving shalom justice in human society. The question of forgiveness addresses the question how to achieve and maintain just relationships in an imperfect human order.[27]

In summary, Jesus' view of God did not set aside the natural and moral order of the universe or minimize the real consequences of social evil. Physical harm or violence such as dishonesty, selfish manipulation, and abuse of others that violates their humanity causes real and morally offensive suffering and hostility. Rather, in the place of retaliatory justice, which attempts to balance harm done with compensatory penalty, he emphasized the intrinsic consequences of evil as alienation, which require reconciliation. Where the inherent wickedness of evil behavior is assessed in terms of its malicious consequences, justice is conceived as that which remedies the wrong done, not as punitive retaliation. John's word that God is "faithful and *just*" in forgiving (1 John 1:9) correctly represents Jesus. God's justice is not demonstrated in following legal formulas for balanced requital, but in the creation of reconciliation and shalom.

Although Jesus did not address the issues of systemic justice in a programmatic way, the idea that shalom justice can only be achieved through forgiveness and reconciliation, which is at the heart of his life and message, is intrinsic to Christian peacemaking. Jesus nowhere spells out a political process of forgiveness in the public sphere as, for example, in the transition from apartheid to justice in South Africa. But as Daniel Philpott observes,

> It is in fact Christian theologians who have most explicitly, vigorously, and systematically argued for bringing reconciliation into politics. . . . Muslims,

Jews, and members of other faiths, although not as many, have also propounded the concept.[28]

This is quite understandable.

Chapter 6

JESUS, LAW, AND JUSTICE

As I point out below, although Jesus' ministry differs from that of John the Baptizer's in both style and deed, he seems to have shared John's assumptions about the necessity of coercive governance, which are implied in his exhortation to the crowds who came to be baptized (Luke 3:10-14). And from Jesus' own teaching and example it appears that love may involve one in coercive actions but never in violence. It is at this point that the nonviolent example and teaching of Jesus most directly impact the social responsibility of his followers in a democracy.

If we are called upon to be as "wise as serpents and harmless as doves" in a violent world, how shall we negotiate such a nonviolent stance? What is the role of law? And how is justice to be maintained? The question can be framed this way: The very concept of law implies coercion. Does Jesus' proscription of resistance to evil (Matt. 5:38) disallow all use of coercion to his nonviolent followers? Some absolute pacifists have maintained that his "resist not evil" does imply this. Is there a legitimate moral distinction between coercion and violence? And if so, where does coercive force end and violence begin in the maintenance of a just social order, such as is implied in the "kingdom of God?"

JESUS AND MOSAIC TRADITION

To get a perspective on Jesus' view of law and its coercive implications, we need to remind ourselves again that Jesus stands in the great tradition of the Hebrew prophets and claims to be the fulfillment of the Mosaic Torah. These furnish the cultural milieu and assumptions from which he operates. The prophetic and priestly interpretations of Torah provide the base for developing his own understanding of its true intent. And while there may be disagreement on how much his message contrasts to the substance of the prophetic message, it is clear that he disagrees with the nationalistic political assumptions of the current Jewish leaders of his day as well as groups like the Qumran community and insurgents sometime referred to as Zealots.

In most people's minds the Mosaic Law is identified with the Ten Commandments, which are given as ten categorical (apodictic) policy statements that stand at the heart of the covenant relationship between Israel and Yahweh. Like the U.S. Constitution, these commandments spell out the moral and spiritual foundation that supplied the religious basis for theocratic Hebrew society. They do not prescribe how these commandments were to be enforced or what penalties should follow for disobedience.

But as Mosaic Law developed over the centuries, statutory and procedural legislation for the regulation of society and the guidance of the judges who pronounced sentences on offenders was incorporated into the legal system. By Jesus' day the Mosaic legal tradition included a full complement of religious civil legislation that regulated not only the temple system but the everyday life of the people.

This expanded Torah was enforced by a coercive police system under the permissive eye of the occupying Roman army. Torah was not simply "natural law" or moral law describing the general principles by which nature seems to work. Neither was it merely religious taboos defining the moral and spiritual sensitivities of the culture and cultic regulations of the religious hierarchy. Torah included accumulated statutory laws and custom intended to regulate society and by its inherent nature implied coercive enforcement.

Jesus alluded to this coercive system when, in a moment of legal pragmatism, he warned his followers to come to agreement with their accusers on the way to court lest judgment be rendered against them and they suffer the full penalty of the law (Matt. 5:25-26).[29]

Torah expounds a theocratic system of laws defining the terms of the covenant between God and Israel. Its primary focus, therefore, was not on settling individual vendettas. Of course the primal human emotions of individual indignation, anger, and rage were operative, and judges "sat in the gate" to hear complaints and settle quarrels, but these were not the primary concerns of righteousness demanded by the Law. Keeping proper relationship between God and the people was the paramount concern. Because the moral character of the nation was a reflection of the divine character, God's honor and reputation were at stake among the nations when Israel was unfaithful to the covenant. It was this honorbound relationship between God and people that established social norms, defined justice, and set the tone for sanctions.

God was recognized as the ultimate enforcer of the Law. Disobedience, even of statutory law, was understood as sin against God, which produced a toxic pollutant that endangered the whole community. Not only was the community's shalom disrupted, but the integrity of Yahweh's holiness was compromised when *God's* Law was transgressed. Justice was understood as God's right social order, and thus God's honor had been defamed. This determined the nature of the sanctions used to enforce the Law.

In such a cultural setting, infraction of the Law is primarily considered as sin against God. Not only the breaking of religious rules, but crime is considered disloyalty to the covenant and is punished as sin against God. Sin breaks the connection of the nation with God, thus the crimes/sins of the leaders were especially dangerous to the shalom of the people.

The major concern of law, therefore, was not equal justice before the law as in democracy, although that was honored in the law of talion. The social-legal rationale for punishment mirrored the result of sin's primary result, namely, alienation and dishonor. Since in idolatrous or immoral or unjust action the sinner/criminal had dishonored God, the offender should be socially dishonored and excluded, which might mean ostracization, imprisonment, expulsion, or even death (a radical form of expulsion). In this manner the order of society was vindicated (put right), and peace was restored.

The means of determining penalties for societal altercations was more subjective and flexible than in a democratic "rule of law." The retributive law of talion as applied in the local setting was used as a general guide for such decisions. For such cases there was no transcendent immutable standard of justice as represented by the Graeco-Roman blindfolded goddess holding a balance. This helps to explain why the sense of vengeance and vindication loomed so large in the minds of the litigants. At issue was the matter of standing in one's community.

This in brief is the cultural context in which we need to understand Jesus' teaching about nonviolence. His relation to this Hebrew tradition is reflected in the description of the Baptist's transitional role as forerunner to the Messiah. Many in his own generation wondered whether John himself might not be the Messiah, but in Christian tradition he plays a transitional role. He is sometimes referred to as the last of the Old Testament prophets and sometimes as the first to announce the new era.

Luke's Gospel presents him as the martyr herald of the new era who introduced Jesus' public ministry (Luke 3: 10-15), while Matthew considers him the last of the old. While his call for true repentance and transformation reflects the new covenant, his prediction of imminent judgment reflects the spirit of the old. Jesus says that there were none greater than he (Matt. 11:11), but even while praising him, Jesus added that the least "in the kingdom of heaven is greater than he."

John's call for repentance prompted the crowds to inquire of him what behavior modifications this change of mind and heart would require. He replied to the crowds in general that they should share the necessities of life with those who lacked them. Of the tax collectors he required honesty and fairness. And he charged the police ("soldiers," NRSV) to not take advantage of their authority to extort bribes, and to be satisfied with their wages. In this he represents the highest level of moral order under God's covenant with Israel. And the fact that Jesus requested baptism from John "to fulfill all righteousness" [of the Law] seems to indicate that he assumed this social order with its implicit coercion as the ground for his own teaching.

Understood in this way Jesus' call is for a more nuanced application of the Law's intent, and not for a radical renunciation of the principle of law. The Covenant Law (Torah) was considered a gift of God that provided a kind of self-identity for the Hebrew nation, and Jesus showed the highest respect for it. His attitude toward the use of coercion is based on the archetypical Hebrew understanding of law and justice. Agape—respect and compassion for friend or foe as "neighbor" for whom one is responsible—is the ground and requisite qualification for law. The goal of law is to establish a righteous social order and maintain a just and peaceful social procedure. Its sanctions must be morally appropriate with its ends. To accomplish this it must both spell out a fair distributive order and regulate the selfish and vindictive impulses that lead to personal vendettas. And all of this in a non-vindictive, non-vengeful way.

Torah recognizes that *retributive* laws regulating vindictive impulses will necessitate coercive enforcement. Legal regulations operate in a less than optimal situation. But it should be noted that the law of an eye for eye and tooth for tooth was first given as a just limitation of blood vengeance for injury, not as a mandatory sentence (Lev 24:19-20)! Thus the government's judicial function is to maintain peace and justice through the rule of law by means of coercion when necessary but without vengeance. If vengeance is to be had, it is in God's place to retaliate. At this juncture, as we shall see, Jesus' teaching on non-*retaliation* comes into play.

Mosaic Law clearly recognized and regulated the right to coercive recompense for injury. Where retributive compensation for loss in the form of a fine was feasible the judges were to make a fair judgment, and in the case of bodily injury the lex talionis was recognized as a fair standard for coercive action (Exod. 21: 23-25). This does not guarantee that all retributive justice laws will in fact be fair! But note that the retributive amends indicated in the law of equal compensation for damage done implies a non-vengeful, non-*retaliatory* legal sanction. Jesus seems to go a step farther and urges his followers to renounce their right to coerced retribution at the offender's expense. Certainly his own example points us in that direction, and his call to "take up the cross and follow me" is an unqualified challenge to waive all rights to self-vindication.

The Mosaic right to retributive justice further implies the moral right to both judicial and police security for oneself and the neighbor. But how far does this implied right extend? Can the idea of peacemaking include peacekeeping? Does it include the right of self-defense and/or the defense of the neighbor being threatened with injury? Protestant ethicists following Luther and his fellow reformers have assumed that such enforcement is implicitly endorsed in the Jesus ethic. Coercive restraint, perhaps even injury, of the offending person may be for his or her own good as well as that of the community.

But Jesus does not leave us any legal analysis or practical case rulings on this question. Does love of neighbor imply the right to injure the hostile law breaker to prevent harm to the neighbor or self? If so, is the chance of causing lethal injury to be condoned? There is no explicit answer to this question, but the relation of law and love in New Testament teachings indicates the direction the disciple is challenged to take.

Law and Love

Most Protestant theologians, beginning with Luther, have interpreted Paul's portrayal of God's love as *grace and mercy* in contrast to *law and justice*. Viewed as grace, God's love expresses itself in overruling and canceling the law of retributive justice. Interpreted this way, Jesus' message of

God's love is contrasted to the pharisaical legalities of Torah and "works righteousness" and leaves the impression that love supersedes and cancels out law. But this is neither the view of the Hebrew tradition nor of Jesus. And, indeed, it is by no means the only way Paul's writings can be read.

The Hebrew Torah was and is still reverenced by Jewish worshipers today as the gracious gift of God. Torah gave Israel its self-identity as God's people and provided their social and moral structure as a nation. Torah spelled out the nature of justice and compassion which was the basis of shalom, or peace. And scholars of all schools of interpretation increasingly have come to recognize that Jesus' life and teaching must be understood in this setting of first-century Judaism with its reverence for Torah. It is a mistake to identify Torah with cultural specific, legalistic practices of first-century Judaism, and to assume that Jesus rejected Torah as a controlling principle. Rather, Jesus insisted that the love of God and neighbor is the Law's first concern, and that its mandates to this end are eternally valid.

This surely indicates that law and its coercive enforcement should not be contrasted to agape. Rather, agape (compassion) and forgiveness are the humanizing limitations on retributive legal processes. Its specific intent is reconciliation and peacemaking. Love transcends law; it does not cancel it out. As St. Augustine observed, "Love does not preclude a benevolent severity or the correction which compassion itself dictates."[30] The intentional ends of both law and love are the same and, indeed, law functions poorly where love and compassion do not mitigate vindictiveness and hostility. They are like the salt and light that preserve shalom and guide the social order toward its God intended end.

"But I Say to You"

Perhaps the most provocative sayings of Jesus that cast his attitude toward the Law into question are found in the Sermon on the Mount. Matthew records Jesus as elaborating on a number of rulings from the Torah—the rulings on murder, adultery, divorce, false oaths, and the laws of retaliation.

Each of these is introduced with the formula, "You have heard that it was said to them of old ... but I say to you" (5:21-45). Scholars debate whether Jesus is referring to the Torah as such or to the many case-laws that had grown up around the Torah to apply its principles. But some take these sayings even further as a repudiation of the coercive legal sanctions inherent in law, especially in the case of retributory justice. Accordingly, Jesus' followers would be expected to "turn the other cheek" and "go the second mile" rather than enforce the law.

It should be noted that in each case Jesus does not renounce the commandment, but in the spirit of Jeremiah 31:31-32 he further establishes it as a spiritual-moral principle for his followers. His "but I say to you" does not nullify Torah but rather challenges the traditional minimal interpretations associated with it in the popular mind (the "traditions of the Elders"). His most scathing denunciations were not against precisionism but against hypocrisy couched in legalistic pretense of obedience. And even as he raises the standards for those who follow him, he does not revoke the sanctions for their enforcement where necessary.

Jesus clearly had great respect for the Law, which he said will endure until heaven and earth pass away. He said that he had not come to abolish it but to bring it to completion and that whoever broke even one of the least commandments and taught others to do the same would be called least in the kingdom of heaven (Matt. 5:17-20). He recommended its thoughtful obedience to the young man who came seeking the way to live a more perfect life (Matt. 19:16-30). He did not, however, make the law an end in itself. Its purpose is the benefit of humankind, and it should be used as a guide, not as a procrustean legal bed. Even the most sacred Sabbath law comes under this moral convention (Mark 2:27).

His view of law fits with his view of God who is the creator of the natural and moral order of the universe. The "Thou shalt not" of the moral law marks the boundaries where peace and justice are threatened. Political legislation attempts to identify these societal boundaries and provide for their reinforcement when they are threatened. Jesus clearly identified with the prophetic interpretation of the Law's intent and presumably accepted its coercive implications, including its punitive implications, although he never spelled them out as did Aristotle and Plato. Indeed, as we have noted, he cautioned those who demand their legal "rights" to take a more pragmatic, non-juridical approach rather than insist on a coercive court battle. If you lose, he warned, you may expect to suffer the full consequences of the law (Matt. 5:25-26).

Since Jesus consciously set his teachings on nonviolent peacemaking within the Mosaic framework of law, we might expect that the focus of his repudiation of violence is on vindictive retaliation rather than passivity or nonresistance to evil. In the next chapter we turn our attention to his teaching concerning *violence* and *coercion* in the pursuit of shalom. If law implies coercion and Jesus upheld the Law, as we have seen that he does, how shall we understand his teachings on agape, forgiveness, and non-retaliation? Do they prohibit all coercive law enforcement and retributive punishment by his followers? Does a follower's concern for restorative justice rule out any and every form of retributive compensation? How does legal vindictive punishment (vengeance) and the consequential judgment that inevitably results from disobedience to God's law relate in the courtroom?

Chapter 7

"VINDICATION": RETALIATION OR RESTORATION

Jesus' teaching on forgiveness, turning the other cheek, and returning good for evil clearly forbids all *revenge* and *retaliation* in principle. However, punitive terms like retaliation, retribution, revenge, vindication, requital, and even reparation tend to overlap in their meaning, and this raises the question whether Jesus is forbidding all penalty and claims for recompense. Do they cancel out or negate the Aristotelian principle of "proportional" justice even in civil cases? Or might peacemaking even require just retribution to balance and rectify the offense? The growing practice and literature on restorative justice have given new urgency to these questions.[31] In any case, these are the questions that legal scholars are debating.

Today a majority of Christian opinion holds that punitive retribution is necessary to preserve a just civil order and limits Jesus' nonviolent teachings to personal reaction and response. Many individuals who claim to be followers of Jesus seek personal "closure" through retributive, even retaliatory, response to criminal offenses. They apply Jesus' command to forgive "seventy times seven" only to individual personal attitudes and reactions. Indeed, neither traditional Roman Catholic nor Protestant Orthodoxy has interpreted the New Testament ethic as either nonresistant or nonviolent.[32] Martin Luther held that ideally executioners who must carry out public death sentences should be genuine Christians because only they can act in the true spirit of forgiveness.

Orthodoxy has held that to uphold the moral balance of the universe Jesus had to suffer as a "retributive sacrifice." God's justice required the penal execution of Jesus before God could forgive sinners. A half century ago C. S. Lewis, for example, argued vigorously for this classical view of retributivism based on a calculation of "just deserts" as the only viable way to maintain public justice.[33] And some from the conservative Christian right in America have gone the next step and argued that the crucifixion of Jesus justifies the death penalty for criminals since God decreed his death as a penalty for sin.

The peace tradition, Anabaptism and Quakerism, associated with pacifism does not limit Jesus' ban on retaliation to individual personal attitudes and response. But this leaves open the political question how his teachings might apply and what role forgiveness might play in the maintenance of public order. Some call for a therapeutic approach of "rehabilitation" of public offenders. Others maintain that if forgiveness is not to become indulgence of wrongdoing, moral forgiveness must include retributive punishment.[34] Still others call for restorative or collaborative justice rather than retribution, which they tend to equate with retaliation. They equate just peacemaking with the restorative process of reconciliation and forgiveness between victim and offender even in criminal cases.

Overview of Terms

Because the penal terms used in the criminal justice system overlap significantly, we first need to establish a working definition of terms. Even dictionary definitions use the words *retribution* and *retaliation* to define each other. And differences in cultural values, as well as personal feelings and intentions, are also caught up in their usage.

Technically *retaliation* implies revenge, payment in kind—injury for injury, pain for pain. One commonly hears victims say, "I want him/her to suffer as much as he/she made me suffer!" As we shall be seeing, in ancient tribal societies where the law of talion[35] was an established measure, revenge aimed at disgracing and crippling the offender. Excessive retaliation was common as a mark of the victim's triumph and restoration of honor. The laws of Torah allow for but carefully limit this kind of retaliation to equivalent harm requited—"an eye for an eye." Thus justice is satisfied in the satisfaction of the victim's injured pride (vengeance).

Retribution, on the other hand, implies reparation for injury done, and while in our modern systems it may include legal penalty, it does not necessarily indicate revenge. It is usually justified as an act of moral equivalency that recognizes and upholds the seriousness of the moral law.[36] Punitive retribution may be vindictive and retaliatory in spirit, in which case the punishment amounts to retaliation. Thus the overlap in meaning. This overlap is complicated by our present judicial practice of defining both strictly compensatory damages and retaliatory (fines and imprisonment) as retribution. Punishment is added as a retaliatory public sanction to maintain respect for the laws that express and embody community values. The offender is said to receive his/her "just deserts" or required "to pay his/her debt to justice," not to the victim.

In Jesus' teaching vindication (retribution) implies recompense and righting a social wrong or injustice, not vindictive retaliation. But one may well object that there are references to vengeance, wrath, judgment, and punishment in both the teaching of Jesus and his followers. Jesus warned repeatedly that suffering and destruction will be the lot of the wicked. He predicted the destruction of Jerusalem as the outcome of Jewish resistance, and he referred to the terrible suffering involved as "days of [God's] vengeance" (Luke 21:22). He promised that God will certainly "vindicate" the righteous (Luke 18:7), and he warned of the great separation of the righteous and wicked at the Last Judgment and the danger of "eternal punishment" (Matt. 25:31-46).

These seeming inconsistencies have led many to conclude that Jesus' teachings on peace and peacemaking are to be understood as spiritual values that have little or no relevance for the world in which we live. His more radical teachings have been dubbed "hard sayings" and relegated to idealism for sectarian practice. While their radicalism must be admitted, they are often far too lightly dismissed without a serious attempt to understand them in their ancient Near Eastern context before applying them in contemporary Western societies.

In the centuries since Jesus taught by the Sea of Galilee, our Western culture and political institutions have gone through profound alterations that ineluctably change our perspectives on the language of Jesus. Stated far too simply and ignoring the complicated developments of two millennia, the presuppositions that underlie our political morality have shifted from a religious theocratic to a secular base. Our moral context for framing penalties for infractions of the law has shifted from a shame orientation to a guilt orientation and our legal concept of justice from personal adjudication between two litigants to a legal decision that satisfies the statutory legislation. Located in a secular democratic "nation of laws" (simulataneously complexified by the efforts of some to re-christianize the nation), we must reframe Jesus' language to understand his intention. We need to change our perspective from secular Western guilt-oriented cultures, with their emphasis on legal sanctions and the equality of individual rights before the law, to a late antiquity shame-honor-oriented communal society.

Christian theology in the West, especially Protestant theology, has increasingly understood Jesus in terms of its Western, guilt-oriented interpretation of Pauline theology. Guilt is viewed as a violation of *the law* and punishment of the offender as a vindication of the law, not of the person who has been harmed. Jesus' death is understood as a justification of retaliatory punishment demanded by God's law rather than a call to sacrificial peacemaking with one's fellow human beings. His message to turn the other cheek is interpreted as a command to passivity in the face of evil rather than a call to uncompromised respect for the humanity of the adversary.

This change in perspective began early in the church's understanding of Jesus as the movement penetrated into the Roman world, and evidences of it may even be seen in the pages of the New Testament. Medieval Western theology, which developed in the cultural context of Roman and Germanic concepts of justice, increasingly interpreted Paul in legal, guilt-oriented terms and framed its interpretation of Jesus in this perspective. Protestant orthodoxy followed this lead and continued to interpret the peace mission of Jesus in legal, vindictive categories. Peace with God was made through the penal sacrifice of Christ's death. God's justice in forgiving humankind was held to be vindicated by the retributive death of Jesus as the Messiah. There was little emphasis on the significance of Christ's resurrection as the vindication of God's reconciliation and transformation of humankind, which Paul explains in his letter to the Romans. In this manner Jesus' life and message of God's offer of shalom was overshadowed by an emphasis on his cross as a penal sacrifice satisfying the retributive justice of God.

My argument here is that to understand the references to wrath and retribution alongside of Jesus' prohibition to take human vengeance, we need to view him in the context of the Mosaic Law. As we saw in the last chapter, the Torah contains two different classifications of law, namely categorical commands as in the Ten Commandments and statuary legislation or case law. The categorical commands are stated as a covenant between God and the people, and the Deity pronounces judgment on their infraction (Exod. 20:5-6). Such divine judgment is executed in terms of the implicit consequences described as the wrath of God.

The teachings of Jesus concerning peacemaking and shalom assume this theocratic framework. God's covenant of shalom is still categorically demanding ("Love the Lord your God with all your heart"), and the consequences of non-compliance are still inexorable. The language of violent reprisal is still used to describe the critical severity of the consequences. But the human work of shalom building is framed in context of the "second commandment," namely, to love one's neighbor as oneself. It is within the jurisdiction of this command that the restriction of vengeance and retaliation apply.

JESUS' VIEW OF RETALIATION

First-century Jewish society was a traditional culture where status and honor ("face") were crucial. In such collective societies, disgrace and humiliation were powerful punitive sanctions for wrongdoing. Arrogance, which the Greeks called *hybris*, is associated with power, and Scripture often speaks of God's avenging justice as "humbling the proud" and "bringing the mighty low."

In the same vein God's vindication of the poor and vulnerable is described as giving them honor and status—a "name." This is, in fact, the social assumption lying back of the Beatitudes of Jesus who declared that the poor and despised are really the ones honored ("blessed") of God. These categories do not easily parallel our legal and moral categories based on idealistic democratic notions of social equality. So we first attempt to understand Jesus' words as his audiences in late antiquity would have understood them.

Social status, which determined both the worth and power of the individual, depended on heredity, gender, and political clout. Higher status in society depended on one's power and influence. Penalties were not based on an egalitarian evaluation of the individual's worth as a creature in God's image. Social justice was defined as enforcement of the proper hierarchical social order. Penal justice was adjudicated according to one's standing in the hierarchical social arrangement. The determination of a just retribution depended on the status of both the victim and the perpetrator. Thus retribution for slaves, women, children, and non-citizens, for example, was not reckoned on the same scale as for male citizens; and shalom was defined as the maintenance of this traditional social order.

This unjust arrangement of society, of course, is not acceptable in modern Christian ethics and raises the question how Jesus' command to love one's enemies and *not to resist evil* should be applied in our modern democratic culture. The question became crucial during the civil rights movement of the 1960s and 1970s when the distinction between "nonresistance" and "nonviolent resistance" was inescapably introduced. Does Jesus' love command to not resist evil forbid resistance against such inequalities in society? Does it forbid the principle of "noncooperation with evil" in an unjust socio-economic system that demeans and harms fellow human beings? Is the conflict caused by nonviolent resistance to be defined as a violent disturbance of the peace? Or is it a peaceable means to achieve the justice inherent in the biblical concept of shalom?

Martin Luther King Jr.'s introduction of the Gandhian principle of nonviolent resistance raised a new problem for biblical scholars interpreting Jesus' words. How could his command to love our fellow humans, including our enemies, be squared with a command that seemed to recommend passivity in the face of injustice? Should the peacemaker advocate submission to abuse in the social order such as seems to be the case in the New Testament advice to women and slaves to be in submission? Clearly Jesus' words take us beyond the social assumptions of his ancient Jewish/Hebrew culture.

Jesus' view of shalom is implied in his two-fold challenge to the ancient social establishment. First, he challenged the hierarchical structures of society according to which justice was dispensed; second, he rejected retaliation as a legitimate moral and spiritual response to malicious injury.

He himself emerged out of the lower classes, and he freely identified with them despite the criticism of the Jewish leaders. While he was no modern crusader for equal rights, he exalted the status of children and women. He refused to recognize class and social structures in his association with outcasts and "sinners." John Dominic Crossan, who has documented this aspect at length, refers to his indiscriminate and egalitarian association with the outcasts and lower classes—those the religious leaders called "accursed"—as "egalitarian commensality." He instructed his disciples not to organize themselves into hierarchical orders "for you are all brothers" (Matt. 23:8-12). All stand on an equal level before God as judge and vindicator. The implication is clear that laws of social justice were to be administrated the same way for all classes. Shalom is a harmonious relationship between equals under God.

Secondly, he forbade retaliation. The focal passage that highlights Jesus teaching against retaliation is Matthew 5:38-41 where he says,

> "You have heard that it was said, 'An eye for an eye and a tooth for a tooth.' But I say to you, do not resist an evildoer. But if anyone strikes you on the right cheek, turn the other also; and if anyone wants to sue you and take your coat, give your cloak as well; and if anyone forces you to go one mile, go also the second mile. Give to everyone who begs of you, and do not refuse anyone who wants to borrow from you."

In this text Jesus forbids the law of talion for injury as vindictive retaliation and violence. It is hard to exaggerate the amount of scholarly analysis and debate that has been spent on this passage![37] But the translators of the *Contemporary English Version* seem to have best caught the meaning: "But I tell you not to try to get even with a person who has done something to you." From among the various Old Testament texts that condone vengeance as a means to rectifying evil and cleansing moral pollution, Jesus chose Leviticus 19:18, which forbade "taking vengeance or bearing a grudge against one's neighbor." And in the verses that follow he extended the prohibition to include enemies as well as neighbors.

Further, the text is not confined to the lex talionis for injury received but expanded to include the principle of no revenge and holding resentment. The focus is not on passivity in the face of evil ("resist not evil") as many versions translate it, but upon *returning evil for evil*. He does not forbid protesting evil or seeking recompense. He himself resisted the hypocrisy and injustices of the system.

Rather, Jesus calls for prevention of injustice by preemptive love and respect for the opponent and for the correction of hostility and injustice by impartial concern for all involved.

Situating these words from the Sermon on the Mount in an honor-shame oriented social order helps us to distinguish in principle between the violence of retaliation and morally justified coercive retribution. As William Ian Miller astutely points out in his studies based on ancient Nordic societies, malicious physical injury is seldom distinct from wounded honor in a shame society, and retribution in the form of the lex talionis inevitably becomes re*taliation*. He writes

> When the debt is of honor (and in an honor society few undischarged debts do not engage one's honor) the notion of getting even is understood to embody a hostile intention to make the other feel your pain, to beat him down, if not to obliterate him. At a minimum it means you want to make sure you (and others) can *see* he is as humiliated as you were seen to have been.[38]

At the center of Jesus' concern is this vindictive one-upmanship that undermines justice and shalom. The Mosaic Torah limited retaliation to equal "injury for injury" (Lev. 24:19-20), but Jesus ruled it out entirely. Retaliation, or law of talion, is proscribed both in cases of malicious wounding and where individual honor has been offended. In his teaching on forgiveness, Jesus also forbade *vindictive* retribution—"getting even," to satisfy anger, resentment, and demanding "rights." But retributive recompense deemed necessary to compensate the injured or defrauded victim does not seem to be in view.

Put into our contemporary terms, the proper purpose of retribution is just compensation and restoring harmonious relations and equilibrium in society, not inflicting penalties to avenge *rights* (honor) of individuals or to justify the moral seriousness of legislation. From Jesus' perspective the ultimate purpose of juridical justice is to right what has gone wrong in society, not retaliatory vengeance. Where the offense involves quarreling citizens, the goal is reconciliation and restoration of shalom.

COERCED RETRIBUTION?

For peacebuilding the implications are obvious. Where shalom is the goal revenge, insistence on vindictive rights or punitive retaliation is counterproductive. Jesus would even seem to caution against insistence on justified retributive recompense where one's individual rights are involved. The admonition that concludes the passage in Matthew 5:38-42, to give freely to those who beg or would borrow from us without expecting to be repaid, does not assume a capitalistic society and clearly takes us beyond the rules for a social ethic.

This much is clear. He clearly teaches uncompromising integrity, compassion, love for enemies as well as neighbors, and rules out vindictive response to injurious behaviors. But what are the analogous circumstances in our modern capitalistic system where his nonviolent teaching applies? Whether or not coercive civil retribution is also ruled out by implication is arguable.

Ross London of Berkely College, whose career has taken him from practice as an attorney and judicial officer to the classroom, maintains that the proper end of the judicial process is to restore trust in social and personal relationships. He therefore argues for a distinction between vengeful retaliation, which is a "subjective punishment," and legal retribution, which is imposed by the state "for the good of others" and can therefore "be understood as a form of altruistic behavior." London is not expounding a teaching of Jesus, but his judgment, although based on Aristotelian principles, clearly mirrors the pragmatic realities recognized in Jesus' advice for peacemakers.[39]

Most interpreters would agree that Jesus is not elaborating civil laws. His command to forgive seventy times seven, for example, was not given as legal advice to the Jewish Sanhedrin, and certainly not to the Roman military authority. But is he prohibiting all recourse to coercive justice to his followers? Those holding the position of strict nonresistance conclude that Jesus was an absolute pacifist, and his followers should not demand retributive recompense or be involved in the judicial processes of civil or military peacemaking, which use coercive means. Those who understand Jesus to be advocating a nonviolent life style draw the lines differently. All coercive justice is not equated with violence, and Jesus' words are understood as exemplary for peacemakers in a violent world. He cautioned his disciples to be "wise as serpents and harmless as doves." Whether private or public, secular or religious, civil or personal these attitudes and characteristics apply to peacemakers as they navigate the hazards of a hostile environment.

Chapter 8

JESUS AND MODERN PEACEMAKING

Jesus consciously rejected holy war as a messianic option. His whole life and ministry repudiate the use of violence for the promotion of Israel's cause. He refused to join the Zealot insurgency against the Romans, or the Jewish parties with nationalistic aspirations that quietly awaited their opportunity for rebellion against the occupation. In the temptation story he rebuffs Satan's offer to give him dominion over the world's military and economic systems if he would consent to violence (Matt. 4:8-10).[40] In the Garden of Gethsemane when the soldiers come to arrest him, he chooses not to call "twelve legions of angels" to do battle with the Roman legions (Matt. 26:52-53). And at his trial he clearly tells Pilate that he does not rely on human military power to promote his cause.

Certainly none of Jesus' direct teachings or his example justify any use of violence against fellow humans. At most by implication his teachings allow for coercive police action in limiting violent behavior. His comment about war, "They that take the sword shall perish with the sword," is quite pragmatic and accentuates its futility. In Jesus' view peacemakers play a role different from warriors or police and have no recourse to violence. His characterization of them requires more than simply following coercive legal requirements. Peacemakers support and help implement just laws by going beyond their minimal requirements and retributive sanctions. They recognize the limitation of law and, while giving full support to just laws and those who attempt to fairly enforce them, attempt to move the fractured situation toward healing and reconciliation.

All this, but did he teach absolute nonresistance? And how he might have addressed the old moral dilemma of taking one life to save many others is not clear. It is difficult to say unequivocally, since there are no clear doctrinaire statements addressing the casuistic implication that might be involved. His teachings have the character of aphorisms or wisdom sayings pointing to the nature of things rather than rational moral principles or the legal dictates of case law. He taught by example and spoke in and to specific situations and happenings usually in parables. This and the fact that he refused to address public civil questions makes it virtually impossible to develop a universal, absolutist pacifist ethic from his teachings.

So in summary how might we characterize Jesus' perspective on peacemaking? How might his teachings and example located in late antiquity give direction to our attempts at peacebuilding in a modern global technocracy of violence? We cannot simply take texts and examples literally since we are working across centuries of cultural changes. But we should be able to discern authentic analogies guided by the attitude, stance, and distinctive characteristic of Jesus, what the New Testament calls the "Holy Spirit" or "Spirit of Christ," which he promised to his followers as a living reality.

Bridging the Culture Gap

Peace and peacemaking are about the social dynamics of authority and control that create and regulate personal relations in society—how human beings relate to each other in community. They have to do with the politics of community in the broadest sense—those networks of relationships that create community. It is not surprising, then, that Jesus used the then-current metaphors of kingdom and citizenship to characterize his understanding of God's intention for shalom in social relations (see chapter 4). Neither is it surprising that he perceived it as a socio-spiritual relationship and spoke in theocratic terms. He imaged God as king and talked about this social network of relationships as "the reign of God."

In our more secular democratic age, in which at least technically religion and politics, church and state, social and spiritual are carefully distinguished and separated into disconnected activities (amid efforts of some to break down the distinctions, sometimes in the interests of civil religion), peace is also defined in detached socio-political and spiritual categories, and the two become disassociated in practice.

If we are to bridge the cultural gap between Jesus and our modern age, it is necessary to preserve the socio-spiritual character of peacemaking, but judging from church history this seems to have been very difficult to do. The theocratic kingdom metaphor has been taken either too literally as a model for a universal political empire—or entirely spiritualized and turned into a mystical relationship to be cultivated by religious disciplines.

At the one end of the continuum, the kingdom of God has been understood as a purely spiritual and future heavenly reality with no immediate relation to present-day social and political structures. Its temporal manifestation is simply a private, inward spiritual orientation or belief system with little or no relevance for one's social and ethical behavior. The Plymouth Brethren, a sect that arose in nineteenth-century England and has had great influence in American evangelical circles, took this distinction between spiritual and social to its extreme, even refusing to recognize a spiritual ("kingdom") dimension in social action.

At the other end of the continuum is the imperial model of the Roman Catholic and Orthodox Churches—"catholic" meaning worldwide or universal, and "orthodox" indicating a dogmatic control of the universal institution. This model of the kingdom unfolded in the medieval Holy

Roman and the Eastern Orthodox Empires which emerged from the earlier catholic (imperial) model. In it the spiritual and the secular were merged under the dual religious-political authority of pope and emperor, and this theocratic empire was identified with the kingdom of God.

The dissolution of this theocratic pattern in the Reformation period led eventually to the separation of "church" (spiritual) and "state" (civil) as we know it in modern Western societies today. The kingdom is identified with the worldwide institutional church and its world missionary movement of the last two centuries. And in nations like America the democratic state is surreptitiously included with appellations like "one nation under God."

A third understanding of Jesus' metaphor is represented in the monastic and sectarian communities who have literally separated themselves from worldly society to follow the nonviolent way of the cross. Already in the early centuries of the church, Christian hermits and monastics formed separated, disciplined communities to obey the dictates of the kingdom. Other sectarian groups since the Protestant Reformation, groups such as Hutterites, Amish, Moravians, Shakers, Ephrata Brethren, Oneida Community, Amana Community, and more have attempted to unite the social and spiritual by establishing the kingdom of God as a sectarian community. But Jesus neither identified the kingdom of God with an ideal community withdrawn from society nor with a purely spiritual reality.

Although Jesus viewed the kingdom as a real transformational social possibility, he did not equate it with any institutionalized form. It is not a master plan for the institutional church. Neither is it a blueprint for a political world order inspired and constructed by the church as implied in the old post-millennial or modern Social Gospel paradigms. The reign or peace of God is not to be realized as a perfected, nonviolent Holy Roman Empire. Jesus did not instruct his followers to build or bring in the kingdom. He neither called his followers to build a powerful world-wide religious institution through missionary expansion nor to dominate a particular society and enforce kingdom rules in cooperation with the worldly powers. Every attempt to institutionalize the rule of God in this manner has fallen far short of the rubric implied in Jesus' vision of God's reign.

What Jesus seems to have had in mind when he used the metaphor was closer to what the gospel of John describes as the wind or breath of God (*pneuma* or Spirit) enlivening and enlightening the universe, expressing itself in human systems of shalom. *God's "kingdom" or reign stands for the effective transforming presence of God's authority operating in this present world.* It is experienced now as a strategic movement of God in which men and women are called to participate working to establish reconciliation, justice and peace.

Citizens of the kingdom live amid a violent, often self-destructive society as reconcilers and peacebuilders. In the words of the ancient Epistle to Diognetus,

> But while they [Christians] dwell in cities of Greeks and barbarians as the lot of each is cast, and follow the native customs in dress and food and the other arrangements of life, yet the constitution of their own citizenship, which they set forth, is marvelous, and confessedly contradicts expectation. They dwell in their own countries, but only as sojourners....[41]

Jesus summoned his followers to participate in society but to play by a different set of assumptions and rules. They are called to introduce the possibility of a new way to live in the world, in short to be "peacemakers." Using this metaphor, churches are political gatherings (*ekklesiai*) representing this peace movement. In the words of Paul, citizens of the kingdom have a dual citizenship (Phil. 3:20). They live by kingdom rules as citizens of whatever nation-state they may belong to. Thus they recognize the need for social institutions and the coercive enforcement of moral and natural boundaries that maintain justice and peace in present human society.

In the agapeic order of God's kingdom, then, love does not cancel out a structured harmony based on coercion and fair recompense for injury. It seems clear that Jesus recognized law as a minimal expression of agape, and he instructed his followers to go beyond the legal requirements of law. However, Jesus calls his followers to a nonviolent way of living and responding that is not based on the vindictive calculation of just punishment enforced by coercion. Such a stance rules out retaliation and by implication disposes them to be reconcilers

JESUS AND MODERN PEACEMAKING

Perhaps to properly hear Jesus' words in today's world, we should begin with a saying from him that sounds opposite and even contradictory to "Blessed are the peacemakers." Two of the Gospels report that when he sent his disciples into the villages and towns of Palestine to announce his mission, he told them plainly, "Do not think that I have come to bring peace to the earth; I have not come to bring peace, but a sword" (Matt. 10:34). And as we have seen, he warned them, "I am sending you out like sheep into the midst of wolves; so be wise as serpents and innocent as doves" (v. 16). Then he added a description of the hostility, intrigue, persecution, and misunderstanding they might expect to find when they announced the good news of peace.

In this situation Matthew represents Jesus as encouraging them to persevere to the end with the promise that his Spirit will be with them, and that the time of the end is near. When we remember that Matthew is being written several generations after the events of Jesus' life, we may assume that this is also a description of the reception that the early believers had already received in the Roman Empire.

Clearly times have not changed much! The attempt to introduce the "kingdom of God" into the midst of our violent societies still threatens the powers that dominate them. The rich still fear and oppress the poor. The poor still resort to violence to resist oppression. Political rulers still make and enforce rules to serve their own advantage. Religious leaders still champion social regulations that "keep the weak in their place" in the name of sacred tradition. Nobody likes "soft-headed liberals" and "pacifists!" In a word, true peacemakers who refuse to cooperate with the injustices of the social order can at the least expect to be ignored as irrelevant and ineffective, and at the worst to be attacked as misguided, dangerous idealists.

Given this ongoing hostile competition and conflict, what in conclusion shall we say about Jesus' understanding of peacemaking? Does he bring a distinctive perspective to modern peacemaking? What uniquely characterizes his viewpoint? Of course we may expect there to be much similar and overlapping teaching and counsel in the global religious traditions, but what might a Jesus-centered approach to peacemaking have to offer? Although Jesus did not elaborate on the cultural and political implications of his parables and aphorisms, we can draw some fairly obvious conclusions from them.

A profoundly religious outlook

First, his outlook is based on a profoundly religious view of the world and human affairs. Jesus' world took it for granted that religion is at the heart of culture. His self-identity and understanding of human life were intrinsically religious. For him peace or shalom was the result of God's will and activity "on earth as it is in heaven." *Thus peace is a transcendent gift, not a secular achievement.* For him the human discipline of peacemaking stems not from democratic presupposition but from a spiritual grounding in and relationship to Deity. Peacemaking is not a new technology, and peacebuilders do not *make* peace. Like midwives they help with its birthing.

Peacemakers' confidence is not in their own skills but in the faithfulness of God to transform conflict and hostility. Peacemakers, like the angels at Jesus' birth, announce the good news of God's offer of peace on earth. Where it is refused, they have no violent options. This dependence upon divine empowerment, known to Christians as the power of the resurrection, is the basis of radical nonviolence. And it is this element of vulnerability that differentiates peacemaking in the Jesus tradition from power-based negotiations at the political peace table.

Nonviolent voluntary service program

Second, Jesus' agenda for peacemaking included a thoroughly nonviolent voluntary service program (Matt. 10:8ff). His representatives were to cure the sick, raise the dead, cleanse the lepers, and cast out demons. That is, they were to share in his own ministry of shalom, bringing well-being to the towns and villages. In contrast to the itinerant magicians, healers, and medicine men who roamed the empire offering their services for a fee, Jesus' followers were to implement shalom without pay. Even so, "wise as serpents" (v. 17), they were not naïvely to think that therefore they would automatically be warmly accepted. Proactive service was to be the ground and hallmark of their peacemaking.

Focus on the vulnerable

Third, we need to note the significance of Jesus' focus on the vulnerable in society, the "victims" of systemic injustice and violence. In the synagogue of his home town Jesus announced that he had come to preach good news "to the poor." In our culture of over-abundance, we tend to associate the poor with a poverty of things. But in the hierarchical society of first-century Palestine, the poor were those without status, those who lived in a perpetual state of victimhood a notch above slavery. These are the classes with whom Jesus identified and associated. His peacemaking efforts were not aimed at policing the power elite but focused in a ministry of healing among the underdogs of society. These lowest in the social pecking order he addressed as the blessed, or honored of God (Luke 6:20), and in the Beatitudes that follow he painted a portrait of the true peacemakers.

These "multitudes" to which he ministered lived in a constant state of what we now label trauma, and Jesus' ministry to them was a healing one. *Sodzo*, which is translated to save, means to heal, and his ministry of peacemaking might very well be characterized as *trauma healing*. His teachings to forgive, act prudently, share compassionately and generously were basic to their healing. Modern interpretations of Jesus' ministry that emphasize the miraculous physical cures usually overlook this essential aspect of healing.

Trauma means woundedness or injury. Feelings of threat, terror, and helplessness challenge our sense of security and control leaving us vulnerable and afraid. Such feelings result not only from the shock of catastrophic events but also from systemic abuse and injustice that deprives people of their ability to meet basic needs. For the "poor" masses with whom Jesus identified, life was experienced as a daily cycle of systemic violence and trauma. His ministry to these traumatized masses of society becomes the pattern for contemporary trauma ministries.[42]

To deal with such a cycle of systemic violence peacebuilders must address both *passive* as well as *active* violence if genuine peace is to be achieved. Until the resentment, fear, and vindictiveness resulting from inflicted trauma are resolved, there is little hope of transforming the cycle of violence. Much of Jesus' emphasis on personal compassion and forgiveness of enemies speaks to this need. The trauma paradigm must replace the revenge paradigm. Despite the outrage done, the humanity of the antagonist must be respected. We must redefine the meaning of "enemy' as Jesus did.

Surely this focus of Jesus is essential to understanding his meaning of peacemaking. The seeds of new violence are planted in the soil of suppressed anger, fear, and feelings of helplessness. Violent revolutions burst forth from the suppressed anger and fear of the vulnerable "poor." In the drift of human history, the rich and powerful of the earth have always been fearful of the wrath of the poor who are their victims. And the poor have always assumed that the way to achieve justice in society is to get even through violence.

Viewed in this context, Jesus' *shalom-making* was a ministry of the "wounded healer" who healed through transformation. Instead of leading a violent revolution as the insurgents of his day advocated or working at political reform of the oppressing structures, he identified with the poor and attempted to interrupt the cycle of violence. At the same time he by no means condoned the inequities of the system fueled by the selfish anxiety of the politically and economically powerful. This nonviolent peacebuilding from the bottom up is the essential message of Jesus.

Contemporary insights about the relation of trauma and violence point us in the direction of the cross. By empirical experience we are learning anew the significance of Jesus' words from the cross—"Father, forgive them *for they do not know what they are doing.*" He understood that his executioners were, like himself, caught in the violent web of abusive human systems. We are coming to realize that the web of trauma and violence is far denser and interrelated than we have heretofore recognized, and its healing cannot be achieved through the introduction of more violence.

Whose religious paradigm?

Fourth, in our world of competitive religions Jesus' insistence on grounding peacemaking in religious conviction raises the sensitive issue of whose religious convictions supply the ground rules. If peace is not made by damping down the significant convictions of one's religion and substituting a secular value system based on the lowest common denominator, which religious paradigm shall we follow? The assumption that in the end all religions teach the same message of peace seems a bit naïve in the global cacophony of religious dissonance. Does Jesus' teaching and example give us a clue for multireligious cooperation in peacemaking?

Surely we must begin our answer by observing his posture of openness and inclusion toward the foreigner and the socially ostracized. His approach was not one of criticism and judgment but of sharing and serving. He was not jealous of the exclusive sanctity of the temple and certainly not competitive! He had a strong self-identity and God-awareness that was not threatened by those who differed. For example, he did not view the Pharisees as religious competitors but criticized them rather as potential allies for not living up to their own teachings.

Indeed, one can almost describe his attitude in the language of James about "pure religion." To paraphrase, "In the sight of God the Father pure religion is manifest in genuine compassion for those in need, and in nonconformity to the violent spirit of the world" (1:27). God is the Parent of all humankind, not just of Jews and Christians. True faith is manifest in faithfully following God's will for peace. In short, the orthodoxies, cultural ideologies, and cultic practices of different religions are not the crucial markers of true religion but rather, in the words of Paul, "righteousness, peace and joy in the holy spirit [of Christ]." And he adds, "The one who thus serves Christ is acceptable to God and has human approval" (Rom. 14:17-18).

Reconciliation and justice in the social community

Fifth, according to Jesus' vision the end of peacemaking is reconciliation and justice in the social community. As we noted earlier, justice and peace are integrally related in the concept of shalom, which is a just, compassionate order under the rule of God. Justice is not retributive justice as in the Roman tradition, which became the governing concept in Christendom. Its symbol is not the blindfolded goddess holding the balanced scales of justice but the elders sitting at the gates of the city adjudicating disputes. The lex talionis may provide guidance in intractable cases of offense, but wisdom dictates a decision that preserves the shalom of the community.

This view of justice as social well-being, which is clearly the view of Jesus, provides the framing context and terms of reference for the concept of restorative justice. Restorative justice, as Howard Zehr says, requires us to "change lenses," to focus attention on the personal and social causes of crime, which is viewed as a violation of people and relationships.[43] It accentuates the necessity of putting right the broken structure of community relationships that have been caused by the criminal violation. Its emphasis on truth telling and responsibility define the crisis as personal, and creates the possibility of transformation to both victim and offender.

All this is clearly in the spirit of Jesus' own announcement of his mission in his home synagogue in Nazareth (Luke 4:18-19). His good news was for the vulnerable in society—release for the captives, freedom for those caught in the oppression of slavery, sight for the blind. Whether he would have included a proportional punishment beyond fair recompense for the harm done, as Stephen Garvey argues in his article, "Punishment as Atonement," is a debatable question as pointed out earlier in this essay.

Peacemakers are not pacifiers

Sixth, in Jesus' view peacemakers are not pacifiers. They are pacifists promoting the harmony and well-being of the social order. Their task surely includes conflict resolution in the form of mediation and arbitration of private disputes, and one welcomes the advances in collaborative law efforts that offer the possibility of non-adversarial resolution of disputes.[44] But peacemaking also includes conflict intervention, and its concern for compassionate justice and impartiality may cause greater conflict in the short term. Clearly by his own example on occasion Jesus initiated conflictual confrontations with those who abused power and oppressed the vulnerable poor.

Although Jesus' did not directly address the problems of religious and political institutions, he did protest injustice and hypocrisy and his message calls for social change. Accordingly peacemakers are called to take initiative to promote social change where there is systemic injustice—but with the firm conviction that a truly just social order can be accomplished only by nonviolent means. The goal of peacemaking is not to prevent all conflict but to transform antagonistic conflict (combative enemy) into efficient conflict (cooperative opposition). And if need be, following Jesus' example the peacemaker absorbs the violence in nonviolent self-giving. That is the nub of what it means to "take up the cross."

From Jesus' example the primary task of peacemakers is not peacekeeping. Peace should not be equated with social quiescence, and peacemaking should not be equated with "keeping law and order." Peacemaking does not aim to shore up the existing social institutions and maintain a static social order. Its purpose is not the fine tuning of social institutions to make them run more smoothly. Indeed, peacemakers operate on institutional boundaries and risk the wrath of social and political institutions in the cause of justice. Jesus was quite aware that his own movement would cause change and conflict, and early in his mission he anticipated the likely finale to his own career.

Justice and its relation to peace

And finally, the distinctive perspective of Jesus' view of peacemaking involves the meaning of justice and its relation to peace. God's will is the source and ultimate definition of justice, not cultural and political authority; and justice is prerequisite to peace.

In our human limitations, of course, we cannot escape the relativity of accumulated cultural traditions and political definitions of justice. Such relativity is obvious already in the admonitions of Paul to slaveholders and husbands in the New Testament church. But in the Hebraic tradition, which Jesus inherited, there was an ongoing prophetic attempt to distinguish between parochial cultural mores and cultic ritual on the one hand, and fundamental rules of justice that are universal on the other. The Mosaic Torah included both ritual and ethical commands and from the beginning accentuated the ethical. But one observes further a kind of ethical trajectory in the prophetic focus on the priority of social justice over ritual commands.

Jesus underscored and climaxed this trajectory when he put human welfare ahead of the many traditional social codes that carried moral sanctions. Even the Sabbath regulations spelled out by the Jewish scholars and religious leaders of his day must give precedence to human welfare. The essential traits of justice are respect for all human life, compassion for the vulnerable and less powerful, honesty, fairness, and impartial judgment, which Jesus summed up in the two greatest commandments—to love God with one's whole being and one's neighbor as oneself. Although this standard can only be applied within cultural relativities, in itself it is non-negotiable! For Jesus justice as defined by God transcends all these relativities and is prerequisite to peacemaking.

Economic dynamics; social ethnic traditions; cultic religious laws and doctrines; or national, racial, and sexual distinctions, do not define standards of justice. While peacemakers must recognize the relativities of expression in the various cultures within which they operate, indulgence and compromise to achieve peace are, in the end, self-defeating substitutes. Jesus was executed by the Roman and Jewish authorities because he refused to cooperate or compromise with the injustice and oppression inherent in their systems. For him the cross was the result of his non-compromise and non-cooperation with human injustice. In that sense the cross is the symbol of God's justice, which will not compromise with iniquity.

In the Ephesian letter the cross is understood as the instrument for reconciling human enemies to each other through demonstrating what God is really like (2:14-16). That is the ultimate meaning of the cross, and the resurrection signifies God's transcendent endorsement of Jesus' self-sacrifice.

Notes

1. Reported in *The Christian Post*, Colorado Springs, March 24, 06.
2. John Macquarrie, *The Concept of Peace* (Firth Lectures 1972, London: SCM, 1973), p. 37.
3. Gerald W. Schlabach, *For the Joy set Before Us: Augustine and Self-denying Love* (Notre Dame, Ind.: University of Notre Dame Press, 2001), p. 122.
4. To support this move they "*affirm* that the Scripture defines and speaks to the gamut of problems in living for all people in all situations" and "*deny* that any particular realm of human life can be sectored off as the unique province of the theories, practices, and professions of the modern psychologies." David Powlison, "Affirmations and Denials: A Proposed Definition of Biblical Counseling," *Journal of Biblical Counseling* 19 (2000): 18-25.
5. *Narrative Mediation: A New Approach to Conflict Resolution* (San Francisco: Jossey-Bass, 2001).
6. For example, Robert Enright at the University of Wisconsin, who "has pioneered the scientific study of how people forgive others,"analyzes the process in depth from a practioners point of view. See his *Forgiveness is a Choice: A Step-by-Step Process for Resolving Anger and Restoring Hope* (Washington, D.C.: American Psychological Association, 2001), p. 299.
7. *The Wisdom of Sirach*, written in the second century BCE, illustrates succinctly in chapter 15 the theistic assumption and the relation of Hebraic Law and universal Wisdom. By contrast Jesus downplayed the Sabbath commandment and said that wisdom is justified in its actions (Matt. 11:17).
8. *Mere Christianity* (San Francisco: Harper Collins, 1980), pp. 116-7.

9. *The Star of Bethlehem: The Legacy of the Magi* (New Brunswick: N.J.: Rutgers University Press, 1999).

10. Although the concept of hegemony will be clear to those familiar with cultural and political discourse, it may not be immediately obvious that religion and religious world views play a significant role in establishing such control. In his book, *From Violence to Blessing: How an Understanding of Deep-Rooted Conflict Can Open Paths to Reconciliation* (Montreal: Novalis, 2002), Vern Neufeld Redekop explains the significance of politics, language, and cultural assumptions (including religious assumptions) in forming such "hegemonic structures." See especially chapter 5.

11. In Romans 3-4 the Apostle Paul wrestles with this problem of religious hegemony. He grants a historical "advantage" to his own religious tradition in as much as it was the historical forerunner of the new way signaled in the Messiah. But the old cultural advantage did not give Judaism any claim to favoritism with God. Now all who embrace the new way of life offered in Christ are on the same footing. There is no "distinction" (3:1-25).

12. For those who are interested in following this development in more detail Larry Hurtado's *Lord Jesus Christ: Devotion to Jesus in Earliest Christianity* (Grand Rapids, Mich.: Wm. B. Eerdmans, 2003), provides an exhaustive study.

13. John P. Keenan, *The Meaning of Christ: A Mahayana Theology* (Maryknoll, N.Y.: Orbis Books, 1989), p. 43.

14. Alan Kreider, ed., *The Origins of Christendom in the West* (Edinburg and N.Y.: T & T Clark, 2001), p. 46.

15. John Macquarrie, *The Concept of Peace* (London, SCM Press, 1973), p. 15.

16. Thich Nhat Hahn, *Living Buddha, Living Christ* (New York: Riverhead Trade, 2007), p. 73.

17. Thich Nhat Hahn, *Peace is Every Step* (New York: Bantam Books, 1992), p. 63.

18. Thich Nhat Hahn, *Anger: Wisdom for Cooling the Flames* (New York: Riverhead Trade, 2002), p. 35

19. Charles Chatfield gives an excellent two page definition and recent history of the terms *nonresistance*, *pacifism*, and *nonviolence* in his chapter, "Revisionism with a Vision," in *Nonviolent America: History through the Eyes of Peace*, ed. Louise Hawkley and James Juhnke (North Newton, Kan.: Bethel College, 1993), pp. 16-17. Also see Chatfield and Kliedman, eds., *The American Peace Movement: Ideals and Activism* (New York: Twayne Publishers, 1992).

20. Eric Routley borrowed the phrase for the title of his book published by Oxford University Press in 1964. For a fuller treatment of the character and role of Christ see chapter 1 of my *God Our Savior: Theology in a Christological Mode* (Scottdale Pa.: Herald Press, 1991).

21. "The Kingdom of God and the Historical Jesus," in *The Kingdom of God in Twentieth Century Interpretation*, ed. Wendell Willis (Peabody, Mass: Hendrickson, 1987), p. 115.

22. Beginning with the writings of Thomas Hobbes and John Locke in the seventeenth century, theocratic assumptions were challenged in western society. Morality began to be defined anthropologically by rational humanitarian criteria, such as what harms and limits the freedom of fellow citizens. Sin was limited to a religious category, and the boundaries for offensive societal behavior were marked out in legal political terms, not by religious ordinances. Ultimately this led to the secularization of public political theology and through a kind of inversion to the identification of secular freedom as a Christian moral value associated with Jesus. The religious value of nonviolent moral responsibility which is at the heart of Jesus' message was thus turned into secular freedom enforced by violence. Mark Lilla has traced this change in Christian political and moral theology from Hobbes to the present in his remarkable analysis entitled *The Stillborn God* (New York: Alfred Knopf, 2007).

23. *Truth and Tolerance: Christian Belief and World Religions*, trans. Henry Taylor (San Francisco: Ignatius Press, 2004), p. 231.

24. For those interested in following this line of interpretation, I suggest N. T. Wright, *The Challenge of Jesus: Rediscovering Who Jesus Was and Is*, especially chapter 6, "The Challenge of Easter" (Downers Grove: Ill.: InterVarsity Press, 1999).

25. At the end of his argument in *What About Hitler? Wrestling with Jesus's Call to Nonviolence in an Evil World*, Robert Brimlow raises the anguishing question that the Jesus peacemakers must face: "How should Christians respond to the kind of evil Hitler represents if just war theory and supreme emergencies are precluded, and if we live with a different meaning of success?" His answer reflects Jesus' final temptation on the cross: "We must live faithfully; . . . and we must be peacemakers. This may also mean as a result that the evildoers will kill us. Then, we shall also die." Then he confesses, "And I desperately want to avoid this conclusion. . . . I may well trot out every nuanced argument I can develop . . . but I would not be telling the truth or living as I ought and as I am called to live." (Grand Rapids: Brazos Press, 2006), p. 151.

26. *Beyond Retribution: A New Testament Vision for Justice, Crime, and Punishment* (Grand Rapids: Eerdmans, 2001), p. 283.

27. See my *Using Scripture in a Global Age: Framing Biblical Issues*, chapter 6, "Jesus and the Politics of Peace," (Telford Pa.: Cascadia Publishing House, 2006), pp 95ff. for a fuller treatment of forgiveness. In characteristic fashion Jesus does not analyze the psychological and moral nature and limits of forgiveness. For such philosophical, ethical, and psychological analysis in the Christian tradi-

tion see Robert D. Enright and Joanna North, eds., *Exploring Forgiveness* (Madison: University of Wisconsin Press, 1998) for an excellent representative collection of essays.

28. Daniel Philpott, ed., *The Politics of Past Evil: Religion, Reconciliation, and the Dilemmas of Transitional Justice* (Notre Dame, Ind.: University of Notre Dame Press, 2006), p. 40.

29. For a more complete treatment of law in the Bible see W. D. Davies's article, "Law in the Old Testament", in *The Interpreter's Bible Dictionary*, vol. 3 (Nashville: Abingdon Press, 1962).

30. Quoted in Roland Bainton, *Christian Attitudes Toward* War *and Peace*.

31. In his article, "Satisfying Justice—Victims, Justice and the Grain of the Universe," Christopher Marshall reflects astutely on these issues. See *Justice Reflections: Worldwide Papers Linking Christian Ideas with Matters of Justice*, ed. Allan R. Duce (Lincoln, UK: IPCA), Issue 10, 2005. The editor may be contacted at 2 Temple Gardens, Lincoln LN2 1NP, United Kingdom, or by email at justicereflections@hotmail.com.

32. Supreme Court Justice Antonin Scalia explained not only his own view of the constitutionality of the death penalty but also gave an excellent brief review of the traditional Roman Catholic view in a speech given on the Pew Forum on Religion and Public Life (2002). For a similar brief but comprehensive view of the conservative Protestant position see J. Daryl Charles, "Thoughts on Revenge and Retribution," first published *Touchstone* (December 2001), available http://pewforum.org/deathpenalty/resources/reader/20.php3.

33. "The Humanitarian Theory of Punishment," reprinted *Justice Reflections* 71.10 (2005), and Stuart Barton Babbage, "Comments on 'The Humanitarian Theory of Punishment,'" *Justice Reflections* 72.10 (2005).

34. This is the position of Stephen Garvey. But he explains, "Of course it's hard to know exactly what retribution is. When we think of retribution, we tend first to think about revenge, or cruel or excessive punishments, or the talionic injunction to take an eye for an eye, or Kant's final decree that the last murderer should be executed to purge the 'bloodguilt" of the community. As I understand it, however, retributivism means none of these things." ("Punishment as Atonement," *UCLA Law Review* 46.6 (August 1999): 1801.

Jean Hampton, who also argues for the moral necessity of restitution, "distinguishes [it] sharply from revenge," which she understands to be "a hate rather than a moral vindication." ("Correcting Harms Versus Righting Wrongs: The Goal of Retribution," *UCLA Law Review* 39.6 (1992): 1691. See also Jeffrie G. Murphy and Jean Hampton, *Forgiveness and Mercy* (New York: Cambridge University

Press, 1988) for an extended discussion of these distinctions.

35. The law of talion is a translation of *lex talionis*, the ancient Roman term designating "like for like" or exactly the same injuries in retaliation. The same formulation is found in Leviticus 24: 21-22 where it applies to bodily injuries inflicted and to murder—"life for life." Other forms of restitution such as financial compensation were also used.

36. See Michelle Maiese's article, "Retributive Justice," *Beyond Intractability*, ed. Guy Burgess and Heidi Burgess (Boulder, Col.: Conflict Research Consortium, University of Colorado). Posted May 2004, http://www.beyondintractability.org/essay/retributive_justice/.

37. For those interested in pursuing this debate, *The Love of Enemy and Nonretaliation in the New Testament*, ed. Willard Swartley (Louisville, Ky.: Westminster/John Knox, 1992), is a good place to begin. Also Luise Schottroff's "Non-Violence and the Love of One's Enemies" in *Essays on the Love Commandment*, trans. Reginald and Ilse Fuller (Fortress Press, 1978) analyzes the issues involved.

38. Miller, William Ian, *Eye for an Eye* (New York: Cambridge University Press, 2006), p. 18.

39. See Ross D. London, *The Restoration of Trust: Charting a Pathway Back from Crime*, unpublished manuscript, 2007, chapter 4. He quotes Kenneth Haas, "The Triumph of Vengeance over Retribution: The U.S. Supreme Court and the Death Penalty," and others in support of his position.

40. To "worship" the great adversary (*diabolos*) who rules the world of power and violence means to recognize his authority and adopt his way of operating in society.

41. From *The Apostolic Fathers*, trans. J. B. Lightfoot, ed. J. R. Harmer (Grand Rapids, Mich.: Baker Book House, 1962).

42. Carolyn Yoder, *The Little Book of Trauma Healing: When Violence Strikes and Community Security is Threatened* (Intercourse, Pa: Good Books, 2005).

43. Howard Zehr, *The Little Book of Restorative Justice* (Intercourse, Pa: Good Books, 2002).

44. While Jesus himself refused to get involved in the arbitrator's role and settle a family dispute ("Friend, who set me to be a judge or arbitrator over you?" Luke 12:14-15), his advice to his disciples to come to a settlement with their accuser before the case comes to court seems more germane to our contemporary mediation processes.

THE AUTHOR

The life of the author born in 1924 has spanned a century of growing conflict and war including nuclear warfare. Following World War II, C. Norman Kraus became involved as a civil rights activist and in protesting the war in Vietnam. His close contact with the Gandhian movement in India in the 1960s, his activity protesting the nuclear buildup, and participation in the movement for civil justice in the United States spurred his interest in the question of the role that Jesus' life and teachings have played in this ongoing quest for a just peace in our world. How does Jesus impact the practice of conflict resolution interventions, such as restorative justice, mediation, and trauma healing?

Kraus has been a teacher and scholar crossing the fields of history and theology with special interest in New Testament studies. He has lectured and led seminars in many cross-cultural academic and interreligious settings. He has been a missionary, seminary teacher, and peace advocate in Japan, India, and Australia.

His published books include *The Community of the Spirit* (Eerdmans, 1975, 1993), *Jesus Christ our Lord: Christology from a Disciple's Perspective* (Herald Press, 1991), *An Intrusive Gospel?* (Intervarsity Press), and *Using Scripture in a Global Age* (Cascadia, 2006).

www.ingramcontent.com/pod-product-compliance
Lightning Source LLC
Chambersburg PA
CBHW022106040426
42451CB00007B/152